WHAT WE SHOULD HAVE KNOWN: TWO DISCUSSIONS

n+1 RESEARCH BRANCH PAMPHLET SERIES #2

Ilya Bernstein

Kate Bolick

Caleb Crain

Rebecca Curtis

Siddhartha Deb

Meghan Falvey

Mark Greif

Chad Harbach

Benjamin Kunkel

Marco Roth

Moderated by Keith Gessen

Transcribed by Andrew Jacobs

INTRODUCTION

THE FOLLOWING ARE TRANSCRIPTS of two conversations that took place at the offices of *n+1* at 195 Chrystie Street in New York City in the summer of 2007. They were prompted by a desire to give college students a directed guide, of some sort, to the world of literature, philosophy, and thought that they might not otherwise receive from the current highly specialized university environment. They were also an attempt to answer the "canon"-based approach to college study in two ways: by identifying canonical books produced by our contemporaries or near-contemporaries—something conservative writers have always refused to do—and, second, by articulating a better reason to read the best books ever written than that they authorize and underwrite a system of brutal economic competition and inequality.

That, anyway, was the idea.

PANEL 1

███████████████████████████

Ilya Bernstein (Moscow, 1971)

Kate Bolick (Newburyport, MA, 1972)

Rebecca Curtis (Tacoma, WA, 1977)

Siddhartha Deb (Shillong, India, 1970)

Mark Greif (Boston, MA, 1975)

Benjamin Kunkel (Glenwood Springs, CO, 1972)

Moderator: Keith Gessen (Moscow, 1975)

███████

STATEMENT OF THE CASE; FOUCAULT, HENRY MILLER, 99 BEST NOVELS

KEITH GESSEN: When I was a freshman in college, I had a booklet slipped under my door, which turned out to have been from the *Dartmouth Review.* In addition to a list of canonized books, it contained a long essay by a professor saying: Everything you'll learn in college will not be true, it will be fed to you by liberal ideologues, and they will try to get you to read strange things. Here is a list of books that you'd be much better off with. And this essay made a very deep impression on me, and it affected the way I studied in college.

I feel like we need to create a counter-text and a kind of supplementary list for young people who are heading to college, in which we tell them what they might read, what we wish we had read, and how we have changed our mind about things.

I'd propose three categories. The first is books that you read too late. The next is books that you mistakenly read instead of reading other books. And the third category of regret is the lack of certain information, which might have come from books and might have come from life, that would have changed some decisions that you made.

I'll start. The first category is "Books we should have read earlier." For me, one thinker I should have read earlier is Foucault. In a way I did read him, I was given him as a sophomore. And I partly blame my teachers, who presented him to me as a description of the world, the Gospel of St. Michel, rather than a critique of the world. And I was not ready for this as a description of the world.

KATE BOLICK: Which book or essay?

KEITH GESSEN: I could not tell you—probably *History of Sexuality*, then "What is an Author?" I was not ready to be told that one's mother is simply a mother-function, and that a writer of books, which is what I wanted to be, is an author-function. That an author is really just a way for literary historians to organize texts.

I wish somebody had told me that this is not the way things are in fact, that this is a radical *critique* of the way things are. And I might have been able to handle it better.

MARK GREIF: How did the *Dartmouth Review* pamphlet trouble you in college, and what was the reading list?

KEITH GESSEN: It was just a list of classics, and I like the classics, but when I was presented with Foucault, I thought, "This is just the newfangled stuff, this is just fashionable, whereas this stuff the *Dartmouth Review* told me to read"—not that I was reading it, but I knew that it was out there—"is the real stuff."

BENJAMIN KUNKEL: You were, like, haunted by the canon.

KEITH GESSEN: I was haunted by the canon.

MARK GREIF: You took the *Dartmouth Review* pamphlet as gospel when you read it?

KEITH GESSEN: I did, because I didn't have any other. The place where I went to college was highly specialized. I don't think there was an idea of a humanistic education, of forming people. There was an idea, as exemplified by the core curriculum, that there are certain approaches to knowledge, and we will expose you to them one by one, but we will not try to form a self out of you. Whereas the *Dartmouth Review* spoke directly to that need to form a self.

Also, I tried to think of a novelist that I should have read. And the only one I could come up with was Henry Miller.

ILYA BERNSTEIN: Hey, that's the one I came up with!

KEITH GESSEN: Really?

ILYA BERNSTEIN: Only I thought not in college, but, like, at age 13.

KEITH GESSEN: Really?

ILYA BERNSTEIN: Yeah, when I opened up Henry Miller, I thought, "Why didn't I read this ten years ago? I would've loved this ten years ago." I still love it.

REBECCA CURTIS: Which Henry Miller book?

ILYA BERNSTEIN: I like *Tropic of Capricorn*, because it's all about New York. But I like Henry as a guy.

KATE BOLICK: Do you mean that reading him earlier would have changed your life, or just that you'd have really liked him a lot?

ILYA BERNSTEIN: I would have just had some good times . . . I mean—in reading, in reading, not in my life. My life was perfect.

KEITH GESSEN: Do you know why you did not read him earlier?

ILYA BERNSTEIN: Yeah, his prose is a little . . . purple. And I think that that turned me off a little bit. But it has nothing to do with who he is, he just happens to write like that.

KEITH GESSEN: I know that *I* didn't read him because he had this reputation of being so sexy, of having so much sex in his books. So actually we had his book in the basement, and I kept flipping through it throughout my adolescence and finding very little sex.

REBECCA CURTIS: Which one was that?

KEITH GESSEN: That was *Tropic of Cancer.* Not enough sex, not nearly enough. I needed more sex as a teenager. And yet it's the perfect book to read as a teenager, not for the sex, but for . . . why did you want to have read him?

ILYA BERNSTEIN: He was a very sane guy. It was enjoyable to be in his company.

KATE BOLICK: It seems to me that Henry Miller falls into the category of "books as enthusiasms"—books that you are lucky enough to find when you are ready to find them.

KEITH GESSEN: I was 27 years old! I wish I had found him ten years earlier. But also I felt he was doing this thing that I hadn't seen in American literature—or I guess I *had* seen it, you know, in Kerouac, or Ginsberg, but watered down and kind of self-conscious—

ILYA BERNSTEIN: Or Philip Roth—

MARK GREIF: Philip Roth is the person I'm most sorry I read when I was young. It ruined my life.

REBECCA CURTIS: How come?

MARK GREIF: I think I read all of Philip Roth up through *The Counterlife* when I was about 13 years old, and I was convinced I was going to get laid. It was a major preoccupation. But of course, when you're a 13-year-old, you don't know *how* this is going to happen. Philip Roth seemed to make it clear that you become a writer, and then you have sex all the time, and you're ridiculously rich—although that's not really clear in the books—but you can sort of move around freely as you like, and there are always people who desire you, and your job is just to tell awful truths about them but they still love you anyway. So I sort of switched allegiance from Stephen King to Philip Roth at that point, and I was like, "This is all going to be so easy," not realizing that in fact what he was offering was not what life offers most people, and not what it was going to offer me.

And it should be said, too, that in my household, Philip Roth was the logical pinnacle as a literary figure, right? So that, you know, Herman Wouk was a great literary figure, Leon Uris was a great literary figure, Isaac Bashevis Singer was a great literary figure . . . you know, anyone who was a mainstream author who could be sold in a Jewish bookshop was a major literary figure, and at the top of them all was Roth, because you could actually view him in a non-Jewish context. He managed to make it into the Jewish bookstore, but he wrote better than everybody else, and he just assaulted the Jews relentlessly. And so at 13 I read him and I'm like, "God, you can get away with anything" . . . I wish I had never read him.

SIDDHARTHA DEB: What Mark says is very interesting. I was completely free of all these influences, because I think my reading is part Third Worldist and part British Colonial. When I told my wife the American writers that people in college told me I should read, she said, "These were all in vogue in America fifteen years before you went to college," which makes perfect sense—they would've taken fifteen years to hit the Third World. And this was the kind of book you had to read to be substantive, intellectual: J. D. Salinger, *Catcher in the Rye.* It sounds strange, but this is one of the books that people told you about. And I think it was good, it was fine, but I could take it or leave it. There were some books that were very bad. I think a lot of people read Ayn Rand, and I did, too. *The Fountainhead*; *Atlas Shrugged. The Little Prince* was big, and that's a nice book.

If I talk about which writers I wish I hadn't read, I wish I'd read less Romantic poetry—I mean British Romantic poetry—because I think it's a very bad influence on a writer at a young age. I think it encourages you to write badly. It's not that the poetry is bad. It's good later when you're more mature, but I think it's very bad to read Shelley and Keats at that age.

MARK GREIF: Because . . .

SIDDHARTHA DEB: Because it encourages you to write terribly, with a certain verbal excess. I think if you read Blake, you're better off, but you don't really *understand* Blake at that time. He gets more interesting later on, again.

BENJAMIN KUNKEL: *Which* time do you understand Blake?

SIDDHARTHA DEB: Maybe you understand that you're not understanding.

So I think I wish I had not read Romantic poetry. I wish I'd watched less Hindi film. I think a lot of people of my generation were ruined completely in certain intellectual ways by watching Bollywood. And *that* Bollywood was nothing like contemporary Bollywood. It was very romantic. It's like you die, you get shot, or the woman leaves you, you sit in a garret writing music or novels for the next fifteen years getting thinner and more bearded, and this is the tragedy. It's the *Young Werther* phenomenon, and it was very influential. I know people who actually killed themselves, clearly under the influence of Bollywood.

I wish I had watched less of those, because it gave me very definite expectations of what it means to go to a city and to try to write. It means you will meet a woman, and there are only two ways. Either you will madly fall in love, and she'll be very rich, and you'll become very rich; or she will leave you and you will *sink* into utter despair. These are very extreme options. I wish as a counter I'd read more French 19th-century novels for a dose of healthy French cynicism, which takes the same trope of young writer in the city, but is utterly quite cynical about it. *The Red and the Black*. I read it when I was 24, and I wish I'd read it when I was 19. *Sentimental Education*. I wish I had read Balzac.

KEITH GESSEN: Edmund Wilson said that you read *Sentimental Education* as a young man and you don't understand it, because you look for the romance, and it's an anti-romantic book. So it raises the question of whether if you had read it at 19 you would have just not understood it.

SIDDHARTHA DEB: That's always possible, yes. But I wish I had.

BENJAMIN KUNKEL: Kate, I like your category of— what did you say—"cases of enthusiasm." It seems that those are things where you have to rely on serendipity, if serendipity is something that can be relied on. And what you can't do is ask a school to schedule your enthusiasms, exactly. So a lot of the things we're talking about, it's not that they'd be irrelevant to students, but they'd be relevant to their extracurricular reading, rather than to what classes they're thinking of taking.

KEITH GESSEN: But it can happen in the classroom too.

ILYA BERNSTEIN: That's true. If you like a teacher, if you admire or have a crush on a teacher, I would take every class that that teacher offers. I wouldn't stop. Somebody told me to do that in college, and I think that was very wise. And then, I don't know about reading the works of the teachers that you admire—they're often very specialized. They're academic works, so it might not be that interesting. But I would read any book that the teacher speaks highly of or is enthusiastic about. Also, if you discover a book you love, if everything about that book is perfect, and if it has a bibliography, look up all the books in that bibliography. That's how you let your enthusiasm blossom and flourish.

MARK GREIF: See, I think you may be usefully disillusioned by reading the works of the teachers. I always feel bad for college teachers, because students are there who have much more power in their brains and they have youth on their side, and they pick up teachers and fall in love with them and then abandon them, throw them away like bits of trash or crumpled-up paper. But this is what you *have* to do as a student. You read the teacher's work, and you're like, "This person is pedantic and useless and just publishing in academic journals, which have nothing to do with my life." And the process is similar when you fall in love, and you want to read the books that the person you fall in love with most likes. At a certain point, if it's not going to be a lifetime thing, you're gonna be like, "I can't believe that person likes *The Name of the Rose*. This is precisely why I no longer love you." Or even, for that matter, "I can't believe this person likes Nietzsche," you know, "I can't live with a monster like that."

ILYA BERNSTEIN: I think I had this problem in general with literature in school, which is that, to me, reading fiction is all about the tension between the book and you, and the book has to make you want to keep going. If it's assigned to you on a reading list, that tension disappears. So you're not really understanding the book, you're just reading it. I mean the whole thing is about the tension. It pulls you, you know, "Should I drop it? Should I not drop it?"

KEITH GESSEN: Do you believe fiction should not be assigned at all?

ILYA BERNSTEIN: I had big problems with it in college. I only took classes where they read fiction because I was interested in philosophy, and there was no philosophy to be had in the philosophy department.

KEITH GESSEN: Kate, what do you wish you had read?

KATE BOLICK: My regrets center less on actual books and more on college itself. As in, I wish I hadn't gone to a small liberal arts college. But given that I did, my advice to the young people of America, based on what I wish I'd done differently, is: Before you start, take stock of your enthusiasms and your talents, and then prioritize them.

For instance, one thing I did right was not major in English. All I'd ever done was read novels—I was *born* an English major—and I knew that I would never read anything else if I didn't make myself. So I majored in American Studies, and I'm glad that I did, because it gave me a sense of history and context that I never would have arrived at on my own.

Yet it wasn't until I left college that I realized I knew nothing about the history of modern critical thought, or even criticism itself. All I'd done, aside from my American Studies coursework, and some printmaking classes, was write and read poetry. This was great; poetry was the most important thing to happen to me in college. But it made me mad that I didn't even know who Mary McCarthy was until I was 24. There were legions of people who'd actively shaped the world in which I was working and reading, and I had no idea who they were.

Which brings me to magazines. That's another piece of advice: I think there should be a little periodicals club, where you meet each month and discuss how people are talking and thinking about stuff in the world you live in.

MARK GREIF: We seem to be on the track of, you know, what if you're going to be an English person, a writer. But what if you're just going to be a human being?

SIDDHARTHA DEB: Or a biologist.

MARK GREIF: Or a biologist. Or a pharmaceutical representative.

ILYA BERNSTEIN: Or an arms dealer.

MARK GREIF: Or a certified public accountant.

KATE BOLICK: It's true. That would be a nice way of doing it, with different lists.

ILYA BERNSTEIN: I think it should be the same list.

MARK GREIF [overlapping]: The same list, yes.

SIDDHARTHA DEB: When I finished college, on the day I gave my last exam, which is pretty much how you finish college in India—there's no ceremony, you just give your last exam and everybody says goodbye in a perfunctory way, and you're not even at your own college, you're at some other college. But there was this little second-hand bookshop I just walked into, and I didn't have much money, but there was this book by Anthony Burgess called *99 Best Novels*, basically 20th-century novels. I had not read much contemporary literature at all. My reading was very, very old-fashioned colonial grab-bag Anglo-Saxon to about 1930. I took this book and basically was very depressed over the next five months. I would go to the British Council library and pick out each one of these books that this man Anthony Burgess had suggested. He had put in a few Ian Fleming books, and he had put in Philip Roth, and Saul Bellow, and I was coming to American contemporary literature for the first time. And it was a very strange experience. I would tick them off, and I didn't go in order, because you didn't know what you were going to find in the British Council library. I read about forty, and then I thought I was healed in some way.

MARK GREIF: Were you healed of . . . college?

SIDDHARTHA DEB: Healed of everything. Romance, college, life, writing, everything.

MARK GREIF: Really?

SIDDHARTHA DEB: Well, temporarily.

CANON WARS REVISITED: HOBSBAWM, HOMER, BUTLER LIBRARY

BENJAMIN KUNKEL: I know a number of people who—what they studied in college they studied because they had some sense that the way people lived in America wasn't quite right, and certainly the politics at large in America weren't quite right, that's to say that both politically and sort of existentially they had radical tendencies. And these radical tendencies led them to study semiotics or something, in which they read more or less fashionable thinkers, some of whom I think have ended up being deservedly canonical, like Foucault. Then they emerged from college, and they still had these radical intuitions, but the radical intuitions were only bolstered by more or less fashionable thinkers, and they felt that their radicalism hadn't gained the authority they wanted it to have. I feel a bit like that. I think a lot of people feel like that.

KEITH GESSEN: Who is somebody you read too late?

BENJAMIN KUNKEL: There are some people I've read too late, and then some people I haven't read at all. I read a fair amount of philosophy, and I wish I had read more. Because I found, as you kind of alluded to, Kate, I can sit at home, and I do sit at home, and read novels. And I'm glad that I studied the English that I did, but not all of it. What I found that I couldn't very easily do was to sit at home and read Kant's *Critique of Judgment*, though I tried, and also I had no one to talk to about it.

MARK GREIF: In this whole big city, you couldn't find someone to talk Kant?

BENJAMIN KUNKEL: That was before my MySpace page. I know some very fetching young Kantians now, I know a number . . . That's not true.

KEITH GESSEN: But name a book that you *did* read, that you wish you had read earlier.

BENJAMIN KUNKEL: Hobsbawm's history of the 19th century.

KEITH GESSEN: *Age of Capital*?

BENJAMIN KUNKEL: *Age of Revolution, Age of Capital, Age of Empire*—it gave me a kind of synoptic sense of what had happened in the world over the past two centuries, what had transformed the world, whether you wanted to call it capitalism or modernity or whatever—and a kind of bird's-eye view of what's going on that wasn't merely facts. He has an argument for what's driving this—which is, of course, capitalism, which is hard to deny—and into this context, into this very expansive context, I could fit the stuff that I knew, and I found that I was fitting the stuff that I knew later than I would have liked.

SIDDHARTHA DEB: Actually, the Hobsbawm books I wish I had read earlier, too.

But I'm not entirely satisfied with this idea of "the great classical thinkers" being handed down. I always think of all those names on Butler Library at Columbia, from Homer to Cicero. And if you go down Broadway to 122nd Street, you'll find that at Teachers College as well. Because if you are at an Ivy League college or liberal arts college, your surrounding is fairly homogenous. You basically come from the same kind of middle class or upper class families. You're not hanging out with the janitors after hours—that's not going to happen. Then when you combine this with the *Dartmouth Review* sort of approach, which is to say, "Look, there's this great Western tradition that stretches down straight from the Greeks, through the Romans, down through the Anglos, to the American empire, and if you know a little bit of this stuff, a little bit of everything, it'll make you feel much better about what you do later on." I simply have no interest in doing anything to support that, and if that's the case, I'd rather they go listen to hip-hop or something, and get their brains mushy.

When I was reading, one question that I often asked was, "What does this have to do with the fact that there's a bomb going off on the street on the next block, and that there are these two groups fighting with each other?"* This was a question that professors had trouble answering. And it wasn't the fault of the text. The text did happen to talk about that in many ways. When you read Shakespeare's *Coriolanus*, you can see a man caught up with a very narrow idea of the classical quality of *virtus* facing what he thinks of as the mob, the plebeians, and how a proto-Fascist figure emerges out of such as situation. So books can speak to the world around you, but how are you going to get them to do this for you?

You shouldn't read fancy critical theory just because it's fashionable. But you need to know what that great classical tradition is doing in relation to the

---

* India in the late '80s saw violent movements along the lines of ethnicity, religion, caste, and class politics, often meeting the reaction of an increasingly authoritarian state.

world. And for that, you need some kind of historical context. Hobsbawm is definitely one of the best if you want to understand this, or something conservative like C. A. Bayly's *Birth of the Modern World*, which I don't agree with, but at least he'll give you a map. And hopefully then you'll start questioning that map, because you won't agree with what he has to say about slavery and Africans being brought here by a kind of equal process or something like that. I'm being slightly unfair to Bayly now. But you need some kind of historical context. It can come from some very good movies. I wish I had seen Pontecorvo's *Burn* when I was younger. I think that would have explained colonialism to me much better as a—

MARK GREIF: What movie?

SIDDHARTHA DEB: *Burn.* With Marlon Brando starring.

MARK GREIF: I guess I should see that.

SIDDHARTHA DEB: It's wonderful. It teaches you a lot that you ought to know about capitalism and slavery and foundations. And it's made during the Vietnam War, so it's about that as well.

MARK GREIF: Hm.

SIDDHARTHA DEB: So I think historical context is important, and as a teacher I get the sense that my students are very, very poorly equipped in terms of historical awareness. They're very bright; they go to a liberal arts college; they're very smart. But whatever kind of historical context it is—world historical context certainly, but even an American historical context—is missing. And I think sometimes the appeal of these *Dartmouth Review* people is that they give a chronology. They give you a timeline, they give you sense of ancestry from—you know, you start with Homer, and then you come to "me," basically. And there's a reason why that has an appeal, in our kind of postmodern groupings of texts lurking around without a context.

BENJAMIN KUNKEL: I wish I'd had the sense that history was still ongoing. Or at least that intellectual history was ongoing. And not just ongoing, but ongoing in the United States. Because I thought, "OK, this is still ongoing in France. And I understand that recently there have been some French people who have thought interesting things." And perhaps some Germans and Italians, too. But, I mean, Mark and I knew one another in college, and Mark had taken a class with Stanley Cavell, and I think that demonstrated to him something that I didn't have demonstrated to me, which was that, you know, an American from

America could be a real philosopher in the world that exists right now.

ILYA BERNSTEIN: Could I say something for a second about the *Dartmouth Review*—and about the vision of the canon that you're describing? The list and the names on the library are basically good names. We could argue about the details, but basically it's a good list. What one has to ask is: Why is this stuff valuable? And I don't think it's so much for the specific content. I think that things that have been around for a long time, things that have somehow managed to get preserved, have enormous value *because* they've been around for a long time. Because there are not many things like that. It's a special category of thing. They exist on these vast time scales. So it's important to be clear about *why* you're interested in those sorts of things. One response is: "Those are our ancestors, that's my lineage, that's my coat of arms." Another is: We have no idea about what the future holds. Everything around us will disappear. The landscape of the future is a complete blank. But these things that have survived from the past—for five hundred years or a thousand years, for whatever reason—are just more likely to survive for another thousand years than anything that we know of. That's it. They survived. We don't know why. And nothing else has survived. So if you want to get some sense of the landscape of the future, it will be a landscape that consists mostly of holes, but it will have some pieces filled in, and some of those names on Butler Library will probably be some of those pieces. And there'll be corresponding names on the Delhi library or whatever. But—

SIDDHARTHA DEB: But there are no corresponding names. If you go through that tradition, then you will have a worldview that will come with it. I'm not blaming Homer or Tacitus for the worldview that is being used now by the people sitting in the US State Department and figuring out how to change the maps. You can read *Iliad* in a number of different ways, and there are many questions about who won, who lost. So it's not the books themselves. But you get a worldview which seems to me remarkably consistent. And in some sense, I admire it for the fact that it is so consistent. It has, in fact, survived the whole onslaught of theory and multiculturalism and remained quite dominant.

I like your argument that they've survived for so long. So much of the world is broken. So much of the past is broken. And it is broken for many more people than those for whom it is joined. It is joined only in this one tradition. If you start cutting it any other way, you will get many more ruptures. I know I'm sounding very postmodern, but I think it's true.

ILYA BERNSTEIN: Let me just make it clear that it's irrelevant to me what civilization you're talking about, as long as it's been around a long time. You can be an American reading Chinese stuff or Chinese reading American stuff.

MARK GREIF: Siddhartha, I keep thinking about the bomb going off down the street from where you were reading Shakespeare. Because it would be my prejudice that if you wanted to understand what's going on with the bomb down the street, if you had read Plato, Hobbes, Machiavelli, Locke, Lenin, and Mao, you would have probably your best chance of understanding very quickly what all the possibilities were for the political structure or theorization that underlay the bomb down the street. It's my sense that even in countries where you'd imagine a long tradition which is different, when it comes to contemporary political action and political violence, people are working within these matrices of available options, of radicalism, democracy, forms of force and of law, which could be taken apart very quickly if you just had that relatively limited political canon. Which would be one kind of argument *for* the *Dartmouth Review* canon, against the spirit of the *Dartmouth Review* canon.

REBECCA CURTIS: Are the canonical texts all part of Western philosophy, or written by Western philosophers?

MARK GREIF: Well, that's the thought. When you start listing philosophers in modernity, it does feel as if once you enter the world of colonial domination, thinkers from colonial countries, too, will be operating within a Western political matrix. So you have to add Gandhi to the list, but once you add Gandhi to the list, it's not as if you're suddenly entering some totally separate tradition, you are, as it were, inflecting or changing the boundaries of the Western political canon.

BENJAMIN KUNKEL: And things work both ways. Because as this Western domination of the world takes place, there's this reciprocal, very unequal exchange, where you get someone like Schopenhauer, leading to Nietzsche, and there's no way Schopenhauer would have been Schopenhauer had he not been exposed to Buddhism. There's no way Thoreau would have been Thoreau had he not been exposed to Indian literature. So I think in various ways, good and bad, the East comes to be incorporated into the West.

MARK GREIF: It's interesting that Leo Strauss, too, is preoccupied with Arabic philosophy.

ILYA BERNSTEIN: I think that our Western tradition happens to have this great memory, and that distinguishes it from some traditions, but not from others. There are other traditions that have great memories, like some Asian cultures. Japan. All those Chinese philosophers. It's a different kind of thing, maybe, but an oral tradition is also a memory. Other cultures may not have such long memories. They may be more patchwork-like when you look at them. That's no reason not to revive them, of course. My thought about students, though, is that, since they have to choose, they have to be exposed selectively. They don't have their whole life. I mean, their whole life is in the future, but they have four years, and they should be exposed to things that are more timeless than less. I would say, read books that are great books. Don't read secondary books—you know, unless the secondary book happens to be a great book. Don't read academic stuff unless it's great academic stuff. Because you're learning, you're being exposed to great things and discovering some sort of enthusiasm in yourself.

SIDDHARTHA DEB: There's a case to be made that in some of the courses really minor stuff gets put in. But I don't know that I have such a benign idea of time. One could argue that reading all these canons, which have been around in the West especially, in the good institutes of the West . . . hasn't stopped their leaders from abdicating all kinds of intellectual and moral responsibility.

BENJAMIN KUNKEL: In fact, it's licensed—

SIDDHARTHA DEB: It's licensed them.

GERMANS VS. FRENCH; JAMESON, ANDERSON, DIALECTIC OF ENLIGHTENMENT

KEITH GESSEN: I want to try to move again to the second question. The second question is—because time is limited in our lives—about books that were read instead of other books. I'll give you an example. I read Frederic Jameson instead of reading Perry Anderson, and this was a great mistake because—

SIDDHARTHA DEB: Which books?

KEITH GESSEN: Oh, you know, Jameson. I read his book on Wyndham Lewis, then I read *Prison House of Language*, then I tried to read the postmodernism book—what's that called?

BENJAMIN KUNKEL: It's just called *Postmodernism, or, The Cultural Logic of Late Capitalism*—

KEITH GESSEN [overlapping]: *Late Capitalism*, yeah. And recently I've discovered Perry Anderson, *Considerations on Western Marxism*, and his many essays from the *New Left Review*. That would have been much more useful to me because Jameson is really trying to enter this tradition, whereas Anderson has produced a historical summary of it.

ILYA BERNSTEIN: Why did you read one and not the other?

KEITH GESSEN: I was just, you know, I thought Anderson was the British Jameson, so why not have the American Jameson? I wasted a lot of time trying to understand what Jameson was talking about.

BENJAMIN KUNKEL: When I was in college there was a kind of either-or fatal choice that had to be made, at least for the type of people I knew. It was this garden of forking paths, or maybe it was more just the road less traveled, and it mattered a lot which path you took. It was either the Frankfurt School or poststructuralism. And I went down the Frankfurt School path.

KEITH GESSEN: What were the steps along this path?

BENJAMIN KUNKEL: There was a class just called "The Frankfurt School." And I'm very glad to have taken that class, although I wish I'd had much more background. I had very little. Here I am, trying to read a synthesis of these strands of thought without having read the original strands themselves, so, you know, *The Dialectic of Enlightenment* was going to be a hard book to read no matter when I read it, but it was brutally difficult to read in my first year of college.

But that choice has really, to some extent, determined the lives of the people I knew in college. There were the people who went French, and the people who went German.

KEITH GESSEN: And what has happened?

BENJAMIN KUNKEL: I think you could quite justifiably complain that the Frankfurt School itself didn't end up being all that political; nevertheless, the political and kind of oppositional cast of thought ended up meaning that people who read them were, in the end, more political. And perhaps they hadn't read any more critical theory for ten years, but one had become an assistant for a left-wing city councilman in L.A., and a labor organizer, and, in my case, an armchair Marxist. An armchair Marxist, rather than an armchair Foucaultian.

KEITH GESSEN: And what happened to those who went French?

BENJAMIN KUNKEL: They ended up being interested more in design and the arts and stuff.

[Laughter.]

KEITH GESSEN: Yeah, I think *The Dialectic of Enlightenment*—that was a major book that I read as a senior. It saved my life.

REBECCA CURTIS: How did it save your life?

KEITH GESSEN: It was a real work of philosophy . . . I mean, it was right on the border between sort of a very long movie review, and philosophy. But it was on the right side, it was philosophy, about contemporary culture, about things that I recognized as being part of the culture that I lived in. And it was the first book of that kind that I read, that was so contemporary, because I *was* pretty sequestered, you know, I was reading the canon, or trying to.

REBECCA CURTIS: "Dialectic of Enlightenment"?

KEITH GESSEN: *Dialectic of Enlightenment.*

MARK GREIF: When I was in college, I remember asking an older person, a graduate student, "What is the single most shattering book you've ever read?" And she said, "Well, *Dialectic of Enlightenment*!"

KEITH GESSEN: And you said?

MARK GREIF: I said, "What's that?"

KEITH GESSEN: And then?

MARK GREIF: Well, it was not for me. I mean, it's funny, that you call them books that are "not for you." No book is for you, until it is. So I looked at it, and I said, "Boy, this book is not for me." And I didn't read it for another ten years.

BENJAMIN KUNKEL: And Foucault, in the interviews he gave for that little Semiotext(e) book, in one of them he said—and someone actually photocopied this and cut it out and taped it to their dorm room door at Deep Springs—"I'm glad that I didn't encounter the Frankfurt School earlier because I know that I would have been doomed to be a Frankfurt School epigone." As in, If I'd read Adorno, I would never have come at this from my own angle and elaborated things that are obviously related, but are not at all identical.

So maybe it was good that it wasn't for you.

KEITH GESSEN: Kate, did you answer the first question—was it Mary McCarthy you should have read?

KATE BOLICK: No, she doesn't mean that much to me, actually. It's just that finding her taught me what a limited idea I'd had of what it meant to be a writer. Back then, I was going to be a poet. I figured that I'd graduate from college and go to an MFA program and teach. Which is a fine way of doing things. But it didn't even *occur* to me that there was another way. I had no critical relationship with what I was reading. I didn't understand all of the different ways of writing, or the different things being written. I simply read for pleasure, and for how my reading informed my creative process. I regret that as a way of reading, but at the same time I don't think it could have been any different. I was a late bloomer! I was coming at things late. And so I always have that feeling of . . . being late.

PHILOSOPHY AND THE LAW

KEITH GESSEN: More choices, wrong book choices?

REBECCA CURTIS: I took classes on single authors, and I feel like I could have done without almost all of Milton, almost all of Chaucer. Like I could have had a little nugget, you know, one week of "This is Milton." I would have gotten *Paradise Lost* from a nice little, you know, "He's on Satan's side, this is the kind of meter he's using."

MARK GREIF: In answer to the question, of reading one thing in place of others, my greatest regret is that I did not read 19th-century German philosophy until much later, and never with the necessary depth. Hegel—German Romanticism, German Idealism—Marx. Once you enter the 20th century, the great lie is that everything up through Kant was historical philosophy, and everything from Wittgenstein forward is not historical, it's contemporary philosophy. But Wittgenstein, the Vienna Circle, Quine, Rawls, Kripke—all of them are historical, and they are most intelligible through history, through their times and social settings.

ILYA BERNSTEIN: Me? I agree with Kate that you come to things at the right time, so it's impossible to second guess. There are things I would have never dreamed I'd be interested in ten years earlier, but I'm fascinated by them ten years later. Because, you know, you sample a lot, your eyes are open, and you really do come to things, at least in my experience, when your interest reaches them. But I'd like to say something about Ben's comment about the roads diverging. This is much more specialized, though. It's not for all "incoming freshmen," it's just for people interested in philosophy. When I came to college, I wanted to do philosophy. And I came to the philosophy department, and all they were doing was logic. I wanted to think about the meaning of life, and this stuff was mind-numbing. So then I looked around, and I saw all these sort of para-philosophies in other departments. The one I ended up in was Comp Lit, where both of these things were read—both the Frankfurt School and structuralism/poststructuralism, the Germans and the French.

So there was this divide between the logical, Anglo-American stuff—which was maybe interesting, but not what you wanted to hear—and then the French and the German stuff, which was what you want to hear. But it was one kind of interesting stuff. What I saw looking back was that there is a great Anglo-American legal tradition that is completely divorced from people who read the Frankfurt School and the French books . . . I didn't know it. I had no idea about this great tradition that exists in the Anglo-American world, as great and intense as anything in any European canon. And it's a thriving, fully living tradition. It's exactly the kind of stuff an aspiring young philosophy major who's interested in the Frankfurt School and Foucault would be interested in.

KEITH GESSEN: Are there people—

ILYA BERNSTEIN: I'm afraid I can't list names, because they would either be in the canon, just sort of generic names, or they would be too specialized, which I'm sort of against. But check out what's happening at the law school, if you're an undergraduate. It's something that the students should get a flavor of. And it hadn't occurred to me when I was a kid to do that, even to look at it. And if it had, I might have seen something I would have become interested in. But it exists. It's rich, the language is incredibly rich. I mean, in the humanities and social sciences, the generic language is horrible, then some people sort of rise above it. But the lingua franca, the standard language, in legal thought, is at a very high level. And it's because they have to watch their language, and everything has to be phrased in the right way. It's an intense tradition, and as I look back at it, that's sort of the great American tradition: the law, and the theorizing around it. That's our Torah, literally. I really think that. You know, like the French have the great novels. That is what we have in the Anglo-American world, and there's a complete divide between that and the interesting stuff—the German and French stuff—and I think that people who become interested in European philosophy will find things of unexpected value in the Anglo-American legal tradition.

MARK GREIF: That's incredibly powerful, what you just said.

ILYA BERNSTEIN: Do you agree with it?

MARK GREIF: I'm *stunned* by it. It never occurred to me, but yes. And I would even add to that. I do think that there's a problem—that were you to go pick up textbooks in constitutional law, it would be less compelling than case law. It's really actually judicial *decisions* which are exciting. And it does offer a living philosophical tradition which is not dependent on logic, and it would be very inspiring to those who are searching for the meaning of life. But, I would simply add—this is something I've never thought about—but in fact, one of the great difficulties of undergraduate education in the United States is that you have no access to either medicine or law, except through predecessor courses which have no connection to the practice of medicine or law.

LIVING AUTHORS

KEITH GESSEN: What would you have done with your life if you had known things you now know? If certain information were available to you . . .

MARK GREIF: I wonder about one more round of books. I just fear that—you know, book lists are so powerful, I feel that that's what we know from the beginning of this discussion. I was just going to say, what if the question were people who wrote in your lifetime. How many books can you name of people who wrote in your lifetime, that the kids absolutely must read?

SIDDHARTHA DEB: The last three decades?

MARK GREIF: Depends how old you are.

REBECCA CURTIS: Fiction?

MARK GREIF: Anything. Any old thing.

KEITH GESSEN: Fiction, we need more fiction.

SIDDHARTHA DEB: We need more fiction.

REBECCA CURTIS: I have fiction. I wrote a list. Should I just read it?

MARK GREIF: Let's do it.

REBECCA CURTIS: Actually, I don't know if these are all from my lifetime. Some of these writers may not still be alive, but—I just read *Enemies, A Love Story*, by Isaac Bashevis Singer. And that was pretty awesome.

MARK GREIF: He lived into your lifetime.

KEITH GESSEN: He died in like '79.

ILYA BERNSTEIN: '89.

REBECCA CURTIS: I think *Blindness*, by Jose Saramago, rocks the world. It's cool because it's otherworldly but doesn't actually contain any impossible events, it's philosophical but plot-driven, kind of psychedelic.

MARK GREIF: I second that.

REBECCA CURTIS: I like *The English Patient* by Ondaatje.

MARK GREIF: Whoa.

REBECCA CURTIS: You hate it?

MARK GREIF: Yep.

REBECCA CURTIS: OK, so it's chick lit.

MARK GREIF: No, it's not chick lit. Lots of people love that book. They're all wrong!

REBECCA CURTIS: *The Lover* by Marguerite Duras. *Invisible Man*, I guess, by Ellison. Is he dead? He's dead.

MARK GREIF: When did he die? Recently?

KEITH GESSEN: '90s. Patrick Giles* used to see him in Harlem.

MARK GREIF: I guess you're right.

REBECCA CURTIS: Let's see. I mean I'm thinking in terms of "must read." I guess I could end there.

MARK GREIF: I just made a quick list. I think, uh—

REBECCA CURTIS: Oh! Leonard Michaels. And George Saunders.

KEITH GESSEN: Really? Leonard Michaels?

REBECCA CURTIS: Yeah!

MARK GREIF: Who is that?

REBECCA CURTIS: Short-story writer.

KEITH GESSEN: OK, go.

---

* Patrick Giles, 1957-2005, literary and music critic. See his tribute to James McCourt, *n+1*, Issue 1. See also www.nplusonemag.com/giles.

MARK GREIF: I believe that it's never too early to start reading Don DeLillo.

KEITH GESSEN: Which book?

MARK GREIF: I hardly know where to start. But I just read *Players* for the first time, and everything he says in there is true for right now. Um, Houellebecq. I think kids should read Houellebecq now—I think they would enjoy it more than anybody.

KEITH GESSEN: Which work?

MARK GREIF: *Elementary Particles.* I actually think they should read Francis Fukuyama. He may be a secondary figure and a summarizer and a neocon, but he's probably the most powerful American summarizer of a whole wealthy tradition, which the kids should know—although they should also disagree with him. And, yeah, Michel Foucault. There's nobody more important in our lifetime.

BENJAMIN KUNKEL: I'd agree about DeLillo, particularly about *White Noise*, which is about a college campus, or set on a college campus. But I think despite this kind of canonical stuff I've been saying, or this regret I've been expressing—at the same time it was very important for me to feel like you could actually grow up and there was intellectual work to be done in the world. One of the things that proved this to me was DeLillo's *White Noise*, because I thought, "Man, this is the world that I didn't know you could actually describe in a novel, and here's someone doing it." And right around the same time that I discovered *White Noise*, I was slogging through Jameson's postmodernism book, which is assembled from various essays he wrote in different places—but some of that stuff, particularly the main essay, was very important to me and still is for the same reason. I thought, "The world is a novel phenomenon, and it's being made anew all the time, and this is someone who's figuring out how to describe that." Someone else I was really glad to read—though I feel that I sort of betrayed him—was [Donald] Barthelme. When did he die? He was writing his best stuff perhaps right before I was born. It liberated me as a writer and made me feel that I could do anything, though I have not yet fully cashed in on that liberatory potential. [Laughter.] But it's there in *40 Stories*.

KATE BOLICK: I'm thinking.

REBECCA CURTIS: Isn't there any more fiction?

ILYA BERNSTEIN: So, DeLillo's that good?

MARK GREIF: Well, it's odd. It's a question of depiction, and being able to describe pieces of contemporary reality that you couldn't do otherwise.

KEITH GESSEN: I think Roth, you know, is more timeless.

BENJAMIN KUNKEL: And yet he harmed Mark.

KEITH GESSEN: I sat down to read *Gravity's Rainbow* the summer after college, because I finally had time to read *Gravity's Rainbow*, but I just couldn't do it. So I decided to read *White Noise*, and that was great.

REBECCA CURTIS: Why couldn't you read *Gravity's Rainbow?*

KEITH GESSEN: It was just too hard. I mean, I read it later, five years later. I didn't really miss much, not reading it earlier. It was OK to wait.

SIDDHARTHA DEB: I think I would put in a couple of fiction names—I would add Sebald to the list.

KEITH GESSEN: Which one?

SIDDHARTHA DEB: All the early stuff, up to *Austerlitz*. *The Emigrants*, *Vertigo*, and *Rings of Saturn*. I would definitely add those three. And I would put Bolaño on my list. *By Night in Chile*; his collection of short stories *Last Evenings on Earth*. I think I would put everything in that's been translated. *Distant Star*, *Amulet*, and definitely *The Savage Detectives*—even though it is a slightly uneven work, I think it's incredible.

BENJAMIN KUNKEL: I think that's the best one.

SIDDHARTHA DEB: It's just amazing. The last two hundred pages . . . [Laughs.]

KATE BOLICK: It turns out that I am constitutionally incapable of speaking for other people, and that's how my reading's been, too. I read fairly idiosyncratically, and I don't think anyone else should necessarily read what I've read. But that said, the experience of reading Virginia Woolf's diaries and letters and novels all at once was a very fun reading experience for me. It was exciting to be able to see and make connections between her thoughts and how those thoughts played out in her novels. So I can recommend that as a *way* of reading.

MARK GREIF: You can't do that with a living person.

KATE BOLICK: Right—

MARK GREIF: You don't have their diaries and letters.

KATE BOLICK: As far as people in our lifetime . . . M. F. K. Fisher isn't one for the ages, but she had a smart way of writing personally that was important for me to read. And Paula Fox's book *Desperate Characters* is a book I still *love*, in a way that other books haven't entered my heart.

KEITH GESSEN: Is it possible you reach a certain age after which books can no longer affect you? True? Not true? True?

OTHERS: Not true!

ILYA BERNSTEIN: Well I have a regret.

KEITH GESSEN: Oh!

ILYA BERNSTEIN: My one regret. I don't regret anything I did, ever. But there is one writer I really regret reading—who is just dreck, but I loved him when I was a teenager—and that's Milan Kundera.

[Laughter.]

I'm ashamed to admit it. When I was 14, I loved Kundera.

REBECCA CURTIS: Yeah, me too. I read, like, three in a row.

MARK GREIF: Why, why—

BENJAMIN KUNKEL: I don't regret it!

MARK GREIF: I don't regret it, either!

REBECCA CURTIS: No, but, I mean, so he's good for you *then*.

ILYA BERNSTEIN: He was good for me then, yeah.

MARK GREIF: He's good for me now!

ILYA BERNSTEIN: It's, it's . . . porn, I think. Not that there's anything wrong with porn—but it's like pretentious porn. And it's sort of a very, very, very watered-down version of Musil, I think. Very watered down. With a lot of sex thrown in.

BENJAMIN KUNKEL: But what a great thing to water down! Kundera was the first person I read that made me realize that essay and fiction needn't be necessarily watertight compartments, that you could do essayistic stuff in fiction. Now, Musil would have proved this to

me, too, had I had the stamina to read any of him—
which I wouldn't have had at 14, I think.

━━━━

AN ESSAYIST'S LAMENT;
MONEY; CLASS

KEITH GESSEN: I want to move us into life choices.
Does anybody regret the profession they have chosen?

MARK GREIF: I have no profession. Whatever profession I do, I regret it.

BENJAMIN KUNKEL: What do you . . . mean? What
are you talking about?

MARK GREIF: I regret it!

BENJAMIN KUNKEL: What?

MARK GREIF: Whatever it is that I've become.

KEITH GESSEN: You've become a philosopher.

MARK GREIF: No philosopher would think so.

KEITH GESSEN: You've become an editor.

MARK GREIF: But that's something to be ashamed of.

BENJAMIN KUNKEL: An essayist? A critic?

MARK GREIF: Essayist! That's interesting. You know, you go through life not really knowing who you are, and one day, somebody calls you an *essayist*. Out of all the pathetic categories that I read growing up, I knew there was no bigger joke than an essayist. Someone who couldn't write something long enough to actually grab hold of anyone, someone without the imagination to write fiction, someone without the romantic inspiration to write poetry, and someone who would never make any money or be published. I'm an essayist!

KATE BOLICK: Sure, I regret, but I also have no idea what I would be other than what I am, so it's useless.

MARK GREIF: That's the problem, that you're doomed. After a certain point. Unless you're firmly taken in hand when you're a small child. And even *then*, you might be ruined, from what you're reading.

[Pause.]

KEITH GESSEN: Isn't there information you wish you'd *had* when you were 20? Siddhartha?

SIDDHARTHA DEB: Yes.

KEITH GESSEN: What?

SIDDHARTHA DEB: I thought I was unique. Because of what I was doing. I know it sounds really stupid, but I grew up in a very provincial place. I grew up in a poorer region of India, and I didn't know anybody who was leaving engineering to go off and study literature. Of course now I know there were thousands of people. I didn't know it then. I wish I had known. Or maybe, I don't know. Maybe if I had known, I wouldn't have done it. Maybe I wouldn't have felt so special. Maybe the difficulties wouldn't have felt so special. I think maybe that's true with all of us.

MARK GREIF: I often say the thing I wish I had known . . . I mean I knew it in some abstract way, but the thing I wish I had known and had been forced home somehow for me at the end of college was *just how much money* people in my classes whom I did not admire or think very much of were going to make once they graduated college.

SIDDHARTHA DEB: Why?

REBECCA CURTIS: Yeah, why?

MARK GREIF: Well, that's the problem. At the time, it wouldn't have really helped me because I wouldn't have believed money mattered.

KEITH GESSEN: Um. *You*, Ben, have written a popular book. An acclaimed book. And a good book, which I recommend.

BENJAMIN KUNKEL: Yes?

KEITH GESSEN: So you must not . . . well, I mean . . . do you feel like Mark feels?

BENJAMIN KUNKEL: I guess for my sake, and for the world's sake, in Mark's case, I'm very glad for Mark's—which was certainly mine too—ignorance of the profound chasm of class difference or whatever that would open up in our later lives. If that's part of what allowed Mark to become a writer. Because it's to the world's benefit that Mark is, uh, what'd you call him? a philosopher, an essayist, rather than a . . . not that he would have been an i-banker anyway. But the kind of economic unrealism of what not just I, but a lot of my friends, planned to do did not occur to me, and I guess I'm glad. I'm glad for that.

[Pause.]

You seem dissatisfied with that.

KEITH GESSEN: Well, it's just I don't really believe Mark. And I wish you would call his bluff.

BENJAMIN KUNKEL: Really? I tried to.

KEITH GESSEN: Do you really feel like you lost your class position when you became a writer?

BENJAMIN KUNKEL: No, no, no. But obviously if you become an intellectual, you stand the chance of forfeiting a comfortable life. I mean, it's a reasonably prestigious field, to be a writer. You have some status. You'll have the status of your class, but you may not . . . you may not have the money.

LAST REGRETS

KEITH GESSEN: Kate, you're somebody who freelanced for a long time, before taking a well-paying job at a magazine. Do you wish you had known ten years ago what you know now?

KATE BOLICK: I see what I'm doing now as a way of redeeming my debts, financially and morally. I couldn't keep living the way I was living.

But again, I only got to where I had to make that decision because I'd had such a poor, vague understanding of what it meant to be a writer. I actually went into writing about books as a way to make money! I thought I'd pay for my poetry with book reviews. It's quaint now to think about. For the record, I stopped writing poetry a long time ago.

SIDDHARTHA DEB: I had no illusions about class or money when I was in college. It was driven home to me very early on. It's painful knowledge, no matter when you come to it, but maybe it's better earlier.

KEITH GESSEN: How was it brought home to you?

SIDDHARTHA DEB: In the Third World, it's very clear. People who have money have cars, and drivers. People who don't have money, don't. The buses are very lousy, and very small.

REBECCA CURTIS: I have a regret. I think that, all being sort of literary here at this table, we're all lucky, since it's hard to support yourself financially as an essayist, novelist, editor, or whatever. I feel lucky to be able to teach and to be able to write fiction. And I love both of those things . . . equally. But I miss interacting with the world in "real world" ways, occasionally, and I wish I'd picked up some side skills. Like even if it were carpentry, or if I were EMT certified, or if I were a part-time fireman. I wish there were something else I was good at, just a little bit. And not for the money, but just to be able to dip into something else, just to re-engage with the . . . the other world, the one that's not the literary world. Almost to perceive it better.

KEITH GESSEN: I had the realization a few years ago, maybe two years ago, that I didn't have any way out. There was nothing I could do, except write, to make money. It wasn't like I had this other thing. It was really the only way I could think of to make money, and if I failed to make money writing—that would be it.

REBECCA CURTIS: But I think you're wrong. If you needed that money, it would be very little time before you could pick up a job as a janitor. If you needed money, you would do whatever you had to.

KEITH GESSEN: OK, last chance to express your regrets.

[Inaudible.]

[Long pause.]

KEITH GESSEN: Last chance for regrets. No?

[Long pause.]

ILYA BERNSTEIN: I do have one regret. I regret having gone to college!

REBECCA CURTIS: Me too!

SIDDHARTHA DEB: I do too. I think it's a waste.

MARK GREIF: It would be much better if you were released onto the world when you were 18, and instead you're kept in this juvenile detention for a further four years, in which you're equipped with things which, frankly, you'd be able to understand much better later—

ILYA BERNSTEIN: I would have done much more if I'd been out of college.

MARK GREIF: And to have an entire nation of people going to college, right? That's ridiculous.

SIDDHARTHA DEB: I think we should go straight to work.

ILYA BERNSTEIN: It was actually like a hiatus in my life. I did stuff before college and I did stuff after college, but what the hell did I do in college?

BENJAMIN KUNKEL: It's summer camp.

ILYA BERNSTEIN: Four years of summer camp.

MARK GREIF: It's like being buried alive, or something, right?

ILYA BERNSTEIN: But you enjoy it.

MARK GREIF: Of course, but you come back from the dead, and you start the chronology over again . . . It's life before and after Christ . . . before and after college. And it shouldn't be like that.

ILYA BERNSTEIN: It was in our power not to have done it, and we all did, so we have nobody to blame but ourselves.

—June 24, 2007

BOOKS THAT CHANGED MY LIFE

ILYA BERNSTEIN

1. James Joyce, *Finnegans Wake* (1939)
2. David Hume, *A Treatise of Human Nature* (1739–40)
3. Edmund Burke, *Reflections on the Revolution in France* (1790)
4. Charles Darwin, *The Origin of Species* (1859)
5. Friedrich Hayek, *The Sensory Order* (1952)
6. Herman Melville, *Clarel: A Poem and Pilgrimage in the Holy Land* (1876)
7. Any movie or radio show by Orson Welles
8. And, of course, J. D. Salinger

KATE BOLICK

1. Joan Acocella, *Willa Cather and the Politics of Criticism* (2000)
2. Maeve Brennan, *The Long-Winded Lady* (1969)
3. M. F. K. Fisher, *The Gastronomical Me* (1943)
4. George Gissing, *New Grub Street* (1891)
5. Vivian Gornick, *Fierce Attachments* (1987)
6. Etty Hillesum, *An Interrupted Life: The Diaries, 1941–43*
7. Larry McMurtry, *All My Friends Are Going to Be Strangers* (1972)
8. Iris Murdoch, *The Sea, the Sea* (1978)
9. Cynthia Ozick, *Metaphor & Memory* (1989)
10. Phyllis Rose, *Parallel Lives: Five Victorian Marriages* (1983)
11. Edith Wharton, *The Age of Innocence* (1920)
12. Virginia Woolf, *To the Lighthouse* (1927); *The Diary of Virginia Woolf, vols. 1–5* (1915–41)

REBECCA CURTIS

1. Nikolai Gogol, *Tales of Good and Evil* (1830)
2. Emily Brontë, *Wuthering Heights* (1847)
3. Marguerite Duras, *The Lover* (1984)
4. Isaac Babel, *Collected Stories*, Morrison translation (1974)
5. Franz Kafka, *The Sons* (1912–19); *The Castle* (1926)
6. Ralph Ellison, *Invisible Man* (1952)
7. Jamaica Kincaid, *Lucy* (1991)
8. Raymond Chandler, *The Long Goodbye* (1953)

SIDDHARTHA DEB

1. Karl Marx, *The Eighteenth Brumaire of Louis Bonaparte* (1852)
2. Eric Hobsbawm, *The Age of Capital* (1975); *The Age of Empire* (1987)
3. Walter Benjamin, *The Writer of Modern Life: Essays on Charles Baudelaire* (2006)
4. Stendhal, *The Red and the Black* (1830)
5. Bibhutibhushan Bandopadhyay, *Pather Panchali* (1955)
6. Roberto Bolaño, *Last Evenings on Earth* (1997–2001)
7. M. K. Gandhi, *An Autobiography: The Story of My Experiments with Truth* (1927–29)
8. Frantz Fanon, *The Wretched of the Earth* (1961)

MARK GREIF

1. Henry David Thoreau, *Walden* (1854)
2. William James, *The Varieties of Religious Experience* (1902)
3. Georges Bataille, *Visions of Excess: Selected Writings, 1927–39*
4. Erik Erikson, *Childhood and Society* (1950)
5. Hannah Arendt, *The Human Condition* (1958)

6. Michel Foucault, *The History of Sexuality, Vol. 1: An Introduction* (1976); *The History of Sexuality, Vol. 2: The Uses of Pleasure* (1984); *The History of Sexuality, Vol. 3: The Care of the Self* (1986)

7. Stanley Cavell, *Conditions Handsome and Unhandsome* (2000)

8. Elaine Scarry, *Dreaming by the Book* (2001)

BENJAMIN KUNKEL

1. Theodor Adorno, *Minima Moralia* (1951)

2. Donald Barthelme, *40 Stories* (1987)

3. George Eliot, *Middlemarch* (1871)

4. Northrop Frye, *Anatomy of Criticism* (1957)

5. Eric Hobsbawm, *The Age of Revolution (1962); The Age of Capital (1975); The Age of Empire (1987)*

6. Javier Marias, *Tomorrow in the Battle Think on Me* (1994)

7. James Salter, *Light Years* (1975)

8. W. B. Yeats, *Collected Poems* (1889–1939)

PANEL 2

Caleb Crain (Houston, TX, 1967)
Meghan Falvey (Bryn Mawr, PA, 1976)
Chad Harbach (Racine, WI, 1975)
Marco Roth (New York, NY, 1974)

Moderator: Keith Gessen

KEITH GESSEN: Welcome to the second roundtable of regrets.

MEGHAN FALVEY: I have a question. I had a hard time coming up with a direct causal line between books and events—even though when I first got Keith's email a few weeks ago, I immediately started to compile a long list. But I don't know that I could say that, having read any of the things that I wish I'd read, that I necessarily would have gone here instead of there, or moved in with this person instead of not, or kept in better touch with my parents.

KEITH GESSEN: You're saying the books you've read have had no consequences for your actions?

MEGHAN FALVEY: No, I think that they certainly did. I'm just curious to hear how we were thinking about what that process of causation was.

MARCO ROTH: It's like after I read *Crime and Punishment* in high school, I wanted to kill an old lady.

KEITH GESSEN: You did?

MARCO ROTH: No. No, I did not, actually. But in that sense, I mean, we can eliminate quixotic causation—

KEITH GESSEN: Well, why don't you give an example of an actual thing that happened from your reading.

MARCO ROTH: Of a book that I read that directly influenced my actions.

KEITH GESSEN: Mhm.

MARCO ROTH: Well, when I was reading Kierkegaard's first part of *Either/Or* in a class on aesthetics at Columbia, the world was filled with love, and I identified with the seducer, and I had huge arguments with my friends about the necessity of indirect communication. And I would *only* communicate indirectly, which later on I realized was just because I was frightened of asking for what I wanted, and I wanted people to give it to me through mysterious and elaborate signals. But that's what being 19 or 20 is like. And then we never made it to the ethical part, *Either/Or*, part II—it wasn't a seminar on Kierkegaard, it was just a seminar on aesthetics.

CALEB CRAIN: I found myself wanting—when I was thinking about this last night—to say a word in favor of regret. When I think back about what I read, and what followed from that, regret was a generative principle. For example, when I was a sophomore in college, I was forced to read Paul de Man's . . . I don't remember exactly which essay, but one of the essays in *Blindness and Insight*, about space, and spatialization of time in Wordsworth—

MARCO ROTH: "The Rhetoric of Temporality."

CALEB CRAIN: That must be it, that sounds right. And I had never read any Wordsworth. I mean, I think I might have read "Tintern Abbey." I had a decent public high school education, but not the, you know, Phillips Andover–style education that Harvard presumed. So I regretted that. I regretted reading Paul de Man before Wordsworth, not least because I had no idea what he was talking about. And also because I didn't have enough emotional attachment to the text. I don't know if it's easy for anyone to follow Paul de Man through an essay, but it was very hard for me, because I didn't know enough about Wordsworth to know whether I cared about what de Man was saying about him.

KEITH GESSEN: Did it ruin the experience of reading Wordsworth when you—

CALEB CRAIN: No, because fortunately I had no memory of it by the time I did read Wordsworth. But a lot of my undergraduate education was like that. In part this was because, like everyone, I went to college at a particular historical moment, which was different—

KEITH GESSEN: What was that moment?

CALEB CRAIN: The late '80s. Which, at Harvard, was the moment when theory was taking over the academy. I was an ambitious person, so I gravitated toward this upstart, small department called Literature, which had set itself up in order to bring theory to the unwashed undergraduates, in contradistinction to the English department, which was standing solidly for reading the texts. It was really only at the end of my education at Harvard that I realized that I would have been much happier in the boring English department, which had resisted theory, because in fact I needed to read those texts. But can I regret having been an ambitious person? I don't think so. You know what I'm saying? I could, but then I would have been a different person, who might not have made much of the English department and the stolid texts, most of which I didn't read until I was cramming for the GRE, and read the *Norton Anthology of English Literature* all in one week.

So I went to graduate school to make up for undergrad. Quite consciously, I went to graduate school thinking, "I'm going to take the sort of courses I didn't take when I was an undergrad and actually learn something this time." Unfortunately, by this time I was at a slightly different historical moment, and theory had finally reached even Columbia—

MARCO ROTH: Wait wait . . . theory reached Columbia in . . . 1976!

CALEB CRAIN: Yes and no, yes and no. When I was taking grad school courses at Columbia in the early 1990s, the tone in the air was, "We're teaching these young people about theory—they've never heard it before!" But I had read all those things already as an undergrad, and when I had to read them all again as a graduate student, I resented them even more. But in a way, I don't regret having read them a second time, because at this point my resentment was so acute that

I was in open rebellion . . . But I have a further regret about graduate school. Because if I'd gotten the education that I wanted as an undergrad, I probably wouldn't have gone to graduate school, and if I hadn't gone to graduate school, I might've just started writing, instead of going into this apprenticeship program for becoming a professor, which I never really wanted to become.

KEITH GESSEN: That's serious. So young people should make sure they get a proper undergraduate education, lest they are forced to go to graduate school.

CALEB CRAIN: But that's the thing. Nobody can get a proper undergraduate education. You'll never know in advance what that education should be. Regret is the feeling you have when you finally realize what the education is that you want. Right? And you're always going to come to that after it's too late. There is always going to be a Henry Adams moment. And so it's not *bad* to have regrets.

KEITH GESSEN: Explain that, the Henry Adams.

CALEB CRAIN: Well, the idea behind Henry Adams's autobiography is that his education took much longer than it was supposed to—took his whole life, really—and near the end he still considers himself uneducated and is still trying to repair the deficiencies. That's a book people should read. But the first time I tried, I got a hundred pages into it, and I was completely put off by his mandarin tone of . . . regret, and sort of fine disillusionment. I couldn't stand it, and it wasn't until five years later that I read it. Which raises another question: It is possible to read books too soon, right? I think there's sort of a built-in protective resistance, at least in my case. If I tried to read a book too soon, I just gave up on it—unless it was for a course, in which case sometimes I still gave up on it.

CHAD HARBACH: Well, Caleb gets everything right. For me, I think regret is . . . you know, it's hard to associate with any book in particular, because regret for me is associated with these vast swaths of wasted time in my past. Years or decades about which I think: What did I ever think, or do, or what happened to me during that time? Caleb talked about Harvard in the late '80s, when theory was coming in, and I went to Harvard in the mid-'90s. And I looked at the Literature department, and it was very scary, and I knew it was too soon for me to read those books. Or, I didn't think that, I just thought it was very scary.

So unlike Caleb, I went into the English department. And the English department at this particular historical moment was—or in large pockets of it—concentrated on atomized close readings, where you take a book or a poem, and you read it in this intense, very narrow way. And this was a sort of game you began to play, and you would become better at this game, and derive pleasure from becoming better at it. But then you go home to your dorm, and you feel very despondent. Because you've learned nothing, and you sort of just feel like your life is . . . you know, I got to Harvard, and I felt regretful about having grown up in Wisconsin and wasting the first sixteen years of my life, so—

CALEB CRAIN: You can't regret something that's not your fault.

KEITH GESSEN: He could have escaped.

CHAD HARBACH: That was what my undergraduate education felt like a lot of the time. And now I've spent ten years trying to make up for it.

MARCO ROTH: Why should we regret anything? You make mistakes, you're supposed to be allowed to make mistakes. I remember existing in this cloud of unknowingness. We'd read theory, and there would be a whole bunch of literature mentioned, and in some ways I feel like this saved literature for me, because then I could go read it on my own, and I never had to deal with anybody talking about it in class, except for the professor. And years later, or it could be months later, but a kind of time lag, you read Proust and you're like, "Oh! I've finally discovered what Deleuze was talking about in *Proust and Signs*." You move through your mistakes toward the absolute . . . Proust is another great author for regret—the purpose of all this retrospection is to redeem your regrets in whatever ways are possible. Why did he spend so much time with the Guermantes? Why did he hang out with anti-Dreyfusard snobs? In order to become Proust.

MEGHAN FALVEY: I was talking to a friend about this, and he reminded me that I once said that the only thing I regretted was real estate. So, you know, not getting a rent-stabilized apartment in a nice part of Brooklyn in 1998 the minute I got off the bus from Philadelphia.

I identify with that story you told, Caleb. Because, you know, our educations take place in institutions that are divided up in these ways that may not bear idealistic close inspection. You can really end up studying the wrong thing, sitting around a table with the wrong people, whose concerns are not your own. Almost inevitably it seems like you won't know what your concerns are until you're older or better read or something. And I too felt, after I graduated from college, that I would just have to go to graduate school.

KEITH GESSEN: Who were those wrong people?

MEGHAN FALVEY: Well, I'll get to that. I remember walking down the hill to my dormitory room after Critical Modern Social Theory, which, along with Phenomenology, Existentialism, and something else with a P—PEP, we called it—were the two major seminars to take at my school for dorks. And so I was very excited to have a place in this seminar, and I was walking down the hill, thinking that I was walking in this mist of, like, glamour . . . the glamour of abstraction. But I don't think I could have given you a description, or really defined all that many terms in whatever we'd read that day. It was probably something like Althusser or that little mean-spirited week we spent on Foucault's *Order of Things*—and he was roundly bashed, which I was very relieved by, because I still find that book impossible to read.

And so I graduated with this sense of just beginning to see what it was that I would find interesting. And I went to a graduate program. I started at one which was essentially a cultural studies program, and those were the wrong people for me. When I transferred to the sociology program where I'm now supposedly finishing my doctorate, I missed so many things. I missed the way people were capable of close readings of nonfictional texts. I missed a certain kind of political involvement. But when I had been in cultural studies, I was definitely approaching real despair. The world is not a text!

KEITH GESSEN: You were too young for cultural studies.

MEGHAN FALVEY: Yeah, I had not read well enough. I had read as well as I could up to that point, but I was just lacking some fairly mundane conceptual abilities, or, you know, familiarity with certain concepts that eventually drew me to sociology, like the idea that you could talk about specific kinds of inequality and their reproduction from generation to generation. Or how getting unemployment insurance has a supposedly dignified status while getting TANF [Temporary Assistance for Needy Families] or food stamps doesn't. And, you know, the irony ends up being that in my department I was considered visibly tainted. I would be the person who says, "But look at that line. Why *that* word?"

MARCO ROTH: So you're too literary for sociology, too reality-based for cultural studies.

MEGHAN FALVEY: Right. And no good at statistics.

o   o   o

EDNA O'BRIEN, JUDE THE OBSCURE, ACADEMIA

KEITH GESSEN: What was the most important book you read in your life?

CALEB CRAIN: *David Copperfield.*

KEITH GESSEN: When did you read it?

CALEB CRAIN: Um, probably when I was . . . 12? And then again, several times, periodically.

KEITH GESSEN: What was the most important book that you read too late?

CALEB CRAIN: Too late. How do you know it's too late? I'm only 40.

KEITH GESSEN: It's always too late!

CALEB CRAIN: OK. I'm embarrassed how late I started reading Henry James. Like, really only in the last few years. I tried when I was younger, and I found it very hard. Now it's like crack. It's not hard to do crack, you know? I can't understand how I ever thought Henry

James was hard. I think your brain changes, and you continue to learn even up to the advanced age of 40.

KEITH GESSEN: Does anybody disagree with that?

CALEB CRAIN: Also *The House of Mirth*. I can't believe that I waited until, you know, I was 37 to read *The House of Mirth*.

KEITH GESSEN: Did you weep?

CALEB CRAIN: I weep every time I read *The House of Mirth*.

CHAD HARBACH: I was just thinking that most of the books I regret not reading earlier were written in the last couple of years. And I regret not having read them ten years ago. James Lovelock's *Revenge of Gaia*, which came out in Great Britain about a year and a half ago, here maybe six months ago. It's very haughty and brilliant, and might be the most excellent and concise book about our ecological crisis. And in a way it probably is Lovelock's best publicly accessible book, but he's been writing these things for like thirty years, so I guess I should regret not having read the earlier books sooner!

The books that one reads tend to take on a sort of naturalness within one's life, so that they seem to come to you when you want them, and when you're ready for them. But then there are questions of expediency. And so for me, the fact that we're on the verge of total civilizational collapse—it could very easily happen within the next fifty or sixty or seventy, at most, years—makes me regret the lateness with which I've figured that out.

MEGHAN FALVEY: I can think of a book that I read too late. I recently found some diary entry from college in which I wrote down, very enthusiastically, an account of an evening spent reading in the common room of this boy who I had an enormous crush on, who recommended Andre Gorz's *Farewell to the Working Class* to me. I ran up the hill to the library after our date and I got the book out and I went back to my dorm room and I read about ten pages of it, and I never finished that book. I'm sorry Professor Gorz, I'm sorry cultural studies. This person and I did read a lot of books in common, and we were together for several years, into my late twenties.

KEITH GESSEN: Even though you never read this book that he recommended.

MEGHAN FALVEY: I don't think he ever read it all the way through, either. I actually, visiting his mother for the first time, saw that she had a copy of it on one of her bookshelves . . . This is what we call cultural capital. But, at any rate, I remember being so dazzled by this person in a way that one really only can be at that age, from inexperience. And part of what dazzled me was certainly my sense that he knew about things that I did not. And there was something shamefully aspirational in the whole idea. I didn't know at the time that you could have a crush on someone who seemed to embody things that you wanted to be yourself. And I read, much later, a not-great novel that told a story set in Dublin in the early '60s, Edna O'Brien's *The Country Girls*, which is a trilogy, the final one being *Girls in Their Married Bliss*—where, of course, there's no bliss to be found. But it's about a very bright but untutored young woman who falls in love with a man, perhaps even a decade her senior, who is an American, who is a novelist and a playwright and, you know, can't even spend that much time with her because he's always going around the world on these fascinating jobs or whatever. And she, it's just so obvious when she leaves him finally that she has simply decided to *become* him, in certain ways, and not in other ways. That her life won't be about struggling to accommodate someone else's ambitions but to pursue her own.

And that was something—both the appeal of making that accommodation and also the fact that I didn't want to—I would not have even permitted myself to say out loud when I was in college. So I think that reading this book earlier, it would have been . . . the similarities and differences between my own experience and the text would have been salutary. I don't know in what ways, perhaps I just would have felt better, and I think that some feelings of things shut down your ability to think, so I probably would have thought better.

CALEB CRAIN: I don't think it's so bad, actually, that book. I liked it.

KEITH GESSEN: That reminds me . . . your description of it reminds me that I should have read *Sons and Lovers* much earlier. Instead I was given *The Rainbow* to read in college, and I hated it. *The Rainbow* is about a married couple, and it was D. H. Lawrence, which is extremely un-literary in a way and sort of alienating—you had to get used to it. So, two steps removed from me: It was not literature that I was used to, and it was about a situation that I had nothing to do with just then, a married couple. Whereas *Sons and Lovers*, that would really have been the thing. So, you know, I read a lot of literature of male liberation, in high school, like *Howl* for example—

MARCO ROTH: Really?

KEITH GESSEN: Yeah. Oh yeah. I loved that. And *On the Road*. You get the Beats—the Beats are accessible to high school kids. But I missed D. H. Lawrence. That would have helped me out.

CALEB CRAIN: I only read *Jude the Obscure* last year, and that was way too late. Because it's brilliant. And it would have spoken to me much earlier—it being a novel about a young person who is an outsider in the culture, but really *wants* to be a scholar, to get inside this magic intellectual place. But because he's an outsider, an autodidact, he gets everything wrong, and he fails in this horrible, heartbreaking way. He spends a lifetime trying to get in, and by the time he understands what it is that he's trying to get into, he realizes he doesn't believe in any of it. That would have spoken to me enormously if I'd read it in graduate school.

KEITH GESSEN: And it would have kept you—

CALEB CRAIN: I don't know if I would ever have finished my dissertation.

MARCO ROTH: I'm trying to think why is it that I persisted in grad school, despite these warnings, like *Jude the Obscure*, which I read in college.

CALEB CRAIN: Oh, you did read it in time, and it didn't help?

MARCO ROTH: No. I'm suspicious of the idea that there's a chairotic moment for certain books, such that they can intervene decisively and successfully. Even after I read *Jude*, I was drawn to the mystery of what's inside the ivory tower, because of course I thought I'd been inoculated or was different and exceptional—and then I realized, the further I went, that almost everyone in academia feels like an outsider, nobody knows what's going on. Academia's an empty vessel, but the ones who don't realize it end up going all the way and end up in charge.

CALEB CRAIN: Who don't realize it's an empty vessel?

MARCO ROTH: Yes. The ones who don't figure it out end up being deans. Or getting tenured jobs. They believe in the system. That there's something they can conform to and master. And the proof is that they've stuck it out while so many others drop by the wayside into "obscurity."

CALEB CRAIN: I can give you some names of books that I wish I'd read because I think I would have enjoyed them . . . Is that something?

KEITH GESSEN: OK . . .

CALEB CRAIN: No?

KEITH GESSEN: Go ahead, yeah.

CALEB CRAIN: I feel like there are all these mid-20th-century British novelists who no one tells you about until you're a grown-up. Like Henry Green, and Ivy Compton-Burnett, and J. R. Ackerley, or Denton Welch, or L. P. Hartley, or Muriel Spark. I feel like they're just pure pleasure. There's this distinction that Richard Poirier makes between difficulty and density, and these are all books that have density, but not difficulty. And the academy tends to prefer books that have difficulty, and not know what to do with books that have density.

KEITH GESSEN: So you would have enjoyed them . . .

CALEB CRAIN: And I think I learned a lot about writing from reading them. They're all enormously stylish writers. But they don't speak to issues. They don't fit into any of the categories that would tend to ferry them into the consciousness of a 19-year-old.

KEITH GESSEN: Which are the best out of those?

CALEB CRAIN: Um . . . *Maiden Voyage* by Denton Welch, or *The Girls of Slender Means* by Muriel Spark, *Loving* by Henry Green, *My Father and Myself* by J. R. Ackerley, *The Go-Between* by L. P. Hartley, *A Legacy* by Sybille Bedford.

■■■■

VELVET UNDERGROUND; SUNDAYS; FARRELL, GALLANT

KEITH GESSEN: I'm going to tell another story about myself. Yesterday I was at the gym, and they were playing something by Lou Reed, sort of late Lou Reed. And I realized that when I was in high school, the song that was presented to me by the radio industrial-capital conglomerate was Lou Reed's "Dirty Boulevard." This was a hit song. And it was a moralistic song about, I guess, prostitutes, and how—

MARCO ROTH: How does it go?

KEITH GESSEN: "Going to end up, on the dirty boulevard/ Going out, to the dirty boulevard/ He's going down, on the dirty boulevard." He's sort of talking it . . . and I—I could tell he was cool, knowing nothing about the Velvet Underground. I was exposed to this, but it was moralistic—this was the song that they allowed Lou Reed to have on the radio, in the early '90s. And I didn't follow up. I could have discovered the Velvet Underground when I was 16, as opposed to when I was 26, and you might say this is a minor matter, but it's a matter of style.

MARCO ROTH: What would have changed? What ways would you have been—

KEITH GESSEN: I wouldn't have been such a stupid idiot, I think, and such a romantic, and such a moralist. And maybe I wouldn't have married so early.

MARCO ROTH: If you had—

CALEB CRAIN: The first four Velvet Undergound albums??

KEITH GESSEN: If instead of listening to "Dirty Boulevard," I had, you know, "Waiting for My Man," on 125th Street.

MARCO ROTH: But you wouldn't have just fantasized about buying heroin, at 16?

KEITH GESSEN: That would have been much more useful.

CALEB CRAIN: I feel like I'm going to ask a personal question. If I shouldn't—

KEITH GESSEN: That's OK.

CALEB CRAIN: Well, were you very moralistic about sex? Is that why you married early?

KEITH GESSEN: That wasn't quite it.

CALEB CRAIN: I mean I was a holy roller Christian when I was—not holy roller, literally—but I was very devout when I was a teenager.

KEITH GESSEN: No, it was just . . . I was very romantic. And I was not cured of this for many years.

CALEB CRAIN: Are you cured of it now?

KEITH GESSEN: Yes.

CALEB CRAIN: What cured you?

KEITH GESSEN: Uh, life. Life had to cure me, and I would rather it had been a book.

CALEB CRAIN: There's something romantic about the Velvet Underground, though.

MEGHAN FALVEY: That's what I was thinking. I mean, the demimonde . . . the romance of getting high and all those things . . . I found very romantic, although I had absolutely no idea where to buy heroin, nor really what to do with it.

MARCO ROTH: What's the lyric in "Sunday Morning" that comes just before "It's just the wasted years/ So close behind . . . " You know that song. It should be the theme song of this particular symposium. You wake up, it's Sunday, what have you done with your life, or week. What do you do with your Sunday—you go out to brunch, you hear footsteps behind you . . . it's just the world catching up, and but it's Sunday, so you do nothing. Because it's Sunday; Sunday's for doing nothing. But *actually*, you know, Sunday is the day to move on from your regrets.

MEGHAN FALVEY: For me Sunday was always the day that I got dragged to Mass, and then, ever since I moved out of my parents' house, it has been the day that I don't have to go to church. So Sunday is . . . nothing can go too bad on Sunday.

But can I interject just briefly? I was thinking, Caleb, when you were talking about the fiction that one doesn't hear about until a certain age. In the past couple of years, I read one novel and a couple books of short stories by two different writers I'd never heard of. Mavis Gallant, and J. G. Farrell's Empire trilogy, I only read them when they were reissued by the New York Review of Books Classics series. There's this cliché quote from C. Wright Mills that the "sociological imagination" is understanding history and biography and the connections between the two. And I really feel like some of the Gallant stories, like "The Four Seasons" or "Gabriel Baum, 1935–()," are almost like case studies of how a person's life will have this kind of feedback loop between their interior psychic life and the forces from above that bear down. This makes them sound didactic, which they're not, at all, they're not like Italian neorealist movies. They're suggestive and subtle in ways sociology can't be. That's not what sociology is for, anyway. But sociology is partly about how people's agency or free will is exercised within limits that they didn't make, and I think people can find that distasteful about sociology, that it can seem deterministic. And sociology also doesn't focus on the individual, and that can seem insulting to people—one doesn't want to "be a statistic," you want to insist on the uniqueness of your life and not have its complexity reduced to variables. So sociologists have to convince people that there's value in thinking this way. And, you know, these books were doing that, in a far more accessible way than even the most popular sociologist.

o   o   o

CATHOLICISM AND THEORY; END OF EVERYTHING

KEITH GESSEN: Were there thinkers that you chose and really followed a certain way down their road that it was a mistake to follow, and you should have followed some other thinker?

MARCO ROTH: I feel like Continental philosophy arguably, to an American, can always be seen as a mistake. And this is what people tell you when you go to college—at least they did when I went to college. You know, they're like, "Don't . . . read . . . Hegel." And of course I was attracted to the forbidden. And the further I went along with it, at a certain point I realized that it would have helped a lot to have had some kind of Catholic upbringing. Which, if you go to school in France, is to some degree the birthright of your educational system.

When they imported this stuff to America, there was no native soil. So you spend a lot of time, you *waste* a lot of time, learning concepts that are really just part of any good Catholic student's high school education. And then you think, when you go back to it: Oh, I just relearned the entire 13th century to read the late 20th century. This esoteric vocabulary isn't even my own, I'm adopting an alien tradition, and there must be some way to speak about this in a language that's my own. And so, this was the great exit from theory that took me until I was . . . 27. I realized the whole project was always like, "How can we translate this into an American idiom that's comprehensible and also teachable?" There're certain American universities where the Catholic tradition is followed very closely, and those tend to have the strongest Continental philosophy departments.

CALEB CRAIN: Really.

MARCO ROTH: Boston College . . . strange places. Notre Dame.

CALEB CRAIN: So what's your regret? Your regret is—

MARCO ROTH: But the thing is, it's not like I would say if I had my life to do over, I would not have wasted my time reading theory just out of an attraction to the forbidden. But I would say that once I figured this out, then I really felt like, "You're stranded," and I could go and remake myself in this Catholic tradition—and many people do it—

KEITH GESSEN: By becoming Catholic?

MARCO ROTH: No, by adopting a theological vocabulary that you don't necessarily have to believe in God or be a Catholic to use. But, you'd really need to go into the whole patristic tradition. And if you do this, Heidegger will become very legible to you. Or, you can kind of go at it in this piecemeal American way, which I never thought really worked. But at that point in my life, I felt I'd reached a limit, and that was my limit. I think limits are different from regrets. You know, sometimes you do things in order to experience limitation.

MEGHAN FALVEY: Having grown up Catholic and gone to twelve years of parochial school, and then having read Heidegger at my Quaker college, I don't think it made any more sense to me than anything else that I read several times over. I mean, it wasn't particularly confounding, but it certainly didn't seem lucid. So, what parts of my patrimony do I not recognize?

MARCO ROTH: I don't know—

MEGHAN FALVEY: Guilt, shame, sin . . .

MARCO ROTH: I don't know, the medieval . . . the tradition of scholastic argument, and St. Thomas Aquinas . . .

MEGHAN FALVEY: I don't mean to like bait you with like, abstract—

MARCO ROTH: No, no.

MEGHAN FALVEY: But I have had that experience, and yet I do not have these concepts. You know, if you're talking about averages, then it might just not be useful to have had your average exposure to things. But Thomas Aquinas . . . I'm sure you know more about him than I do.

CHAD HARBACH: I wish I could answer this question. I wish that there had been some thinker or strain of thought that I had latched onto and taken too far, and, you know, they put me in jail for it . . . and I sat in a pensive state with my intellectual problems, and I came out and I was reborn.

But I guess I feel, looking back over my younger life, I just sort of drifted along from day to day and year to year. I read in a vacuum for a long time, acquiring stuff, without coming up with some sort of useful framework in which to put all that stuff.

KEITH GESSEN: Do you have that framework now?

CHAD HARBACH: I do have that framework now.

KEITH GESSEN: How'd you get it?

CHAD HARBACH: By becoming old, maybe. I think at a certain point—and this may happen very early for some people and later for some people—your education shifts from this sheer accumulation of stuff, to a posing to yourself of certain fundamental questions, and then in certain ways life becomes very easy thereafter.

MARCO ROTH: What are the four fundamental questions!

CHAD HARBACH: For me, at the current moment, the fundamental question is: We're at this point where our civilization is going to collapse, and we as a species and as a planet are about to destroy ourselves, and so from this historical point, there are two questions. One looks back at the liberal, humanistic tradition and says, "How did we come to this point?" And so one begins to read the history of literature, or whatever, through this particular lens. And then one looks forward and says, "Is there anything we can conceivably do to mitigate this?" And in an intellectual way, this is a very rich framework. It's unfortunate that we have only a certain time to work with this very rich framework, because everything's going to collapse.

CALEB CRAIN: So we have to read the right books.

MARCO ROTH: Right away! I mean this is a whole curriculum. If we're at this apocalyptic moment, right, then you just kind of want to discard about a thousand years of civilization, and just learn to get by on what you need for the coming apocalypse. What is the book that people should be reading at the dawn of climate change? I mean, it's not Proust.

CHAD HARBACH: You could read Proust. It's an interesting question. *Walden* is a very important book. But, you know, these problems are philosophical, and psychological, and also economic and scientific, so they don't determine the sort of discipline one should study—

MARCO ROTH: Not English.

CHAD HARBACH: People could study English. It's a philosophical problem, ultimately. And ultimately it requires a philosophical solution. And so none of these disciplines—to me, and maybe I'm wrong—are off-limits, but whatever a person is going to go into, they need a certain fundamental grounding in the primary problems of the time. And the primary problem of the time is that the earth is being degraded far more quickly than we can handle, and we have very few years to do anything about it—probably on the order of single digits, though what we do ten to 100 years from now will also be important. But many of our ideas about the world still seem to come from the field of classical economics, which operates in a kind of vacuum, and which was conceived at a time when an understanding that the earth's resources are finite just was not possible, because there were however many people on the earth, maybe a billion, and there was just ample stuff everywhere. And most of the prominent economists of our time still operate on these same principles. So economics, in a way, is the primary discipline at the moment, because it dictates so much of what we do as a society, and even dominates our language. And it's also the discipline that's the most misguided and needs the most help. Which doesn't necessarily mean that you shouldn't do English, but the person doing English should understand these things that undergird us, which they may not understand from their curriculum.

[Pause.]

KEITH GESSEN: My example from my own life would be that I spent a whole lot of time reading Nietzsche, thinking Nietzsche, two years quoting Nietzsche on every possible thing. And then when I started reading Marx, I was like, "Well, actually, Marx would have done just as well emotionally, and it would have been a lot more useful analytically." But by then it was too late, because I'd already kind of passed the age when I could get really excited—when I could let a philosopher run my life.

MARCO ROTH: When did you—

KEITH GESSEN: When I was 20.

MARCO ROTH: —read Marx?

KEITH GESSEN: Oh. The next year. When I was 21.

CALEB CRAIN: For me, that was Emerson, but I don't regret it.

CHAD HARBACH: You read Emerson instead of Marx?

CALEB CRAIN: Yes, basically. Emerson instead of Nietzsche, I think. Nietzsche kept a copy of Emerson in his back pocket.

MEGHAN FALVEY: Actually, going back to what you said earlier, Marco, about this Catholic Thomist tradition . . . there must be so many ex-Catholics, not just Terry Eagleton and me, who then go on to find Marx powerfully persuasive. You have a total system of explanation that accounts for every kind of phenomenon, if not specifically, then in some abstract way. It's not so hard to move from piety to idealism, or to revolutionary fervor. So, that always seemed highly suspect to me. And I wouldn't say I should have become an obnoxious collegiate Foucaultian instead, but only that I wish I had read, alongside Marx and the people he worked with, I wish I had read more criticisms of it. Obviously Hayek and Schumpeter, and even something random like Raymond Aron, the conservative French sociologist, things like that. It's not like now I see what a sham the stuff I read in college was. But it would have been nice to have not gone from being an embarrassingly pious child to being a sort of vulgar economic determinist in a certain kind of way.

KEITH GESSEN: Is Marx a sham?

MEGHAN FALVEY: Oh . . . How much time do we have left? No, of course he's not a sham. Did I suggest that?

OTHERS: Yeah.

MARCO ROTH: Strike that from the record!

MEGHAN FALVEY: No no no no no. No. It's just that I wish that precisely because the kind of autobiographically determined ease with which I took to the idea that there could be one right system of philosophy which would explain everything about the way the world works for you, and also suggest to you how it might work better—that is, ethically . . . I think the ease with which I did that is something that prevented me from realizing how much I believed it. As opposed to understanding it and using it as an analytic tool. I didn't have any critical perspective on it whatsoever, and I believed it as a total theory.

KEITH GESSEN: I don't think you need to be Catholic to wish for a total theory. Or even young.

CALEB CRAIN: Peter and I were talking about this last night—we both agreed that we regretted reading *Naked Lunch* when we were teenagers. If you're going to be gay, and you read *Naked Lunch* when you're a teenager, then I think it sort of sets you back a few years. Because it's blue in this ultimately cheap way. You know, the whole "snuff flick" passage. I don't think the Gothic is the easiest way to enter into possession of one's homosexuality. If there is to be one book that the adolescents of America read about homosexuality, maybe it shouldn't be *Naked Lunch*.

KEITH GESSEN: What *should* it be?

CALEB CRAIN: It wasn't around when I was a teenager, but I wish that I could have read something like *The Line of Beauty* by Alan Hollinghurst. Conveniently for me, it's about someone my age who came out around the time I did, but in Britain.

KEITH GESSEN: I want to follow up with you, since we have a biographical moment of coming out, which was when?

CALEB CRAIN: For me? Late senior year of college . . . so 1989.

KEITH GESSEN: Were there books that helped with this?

CALEB CRAIN: How could there not be? There was *Moby-Dick*. There was obsessive reading and memorization of long passages of *Moby-Dick*, recitation aloud late at night, to myself, while completely inebriated.

CHAD HARBACH: That's funny, because I did that too.

CALEB CRAIN: Didn't lead to the same place, yeah. But that's the advantage of *Moby-Dick*. It has a broader cultural resonance.

KEITH GESSEN: But how'd that work?

CALEB CRAIN: I don't know if it worked, or if it was a symptom. I felt that I recognized a feeling that I shared. And that was important, to feel like I saw this feeling that I thought was wrong and forbidden, showing up in this great, classic work of literature. Maybe it still was a bad and wrong feeling, but at least it had a little glamour. At least somebody had thought—*many* people had thought—that it had enough importance to enshrine in this classic. That kind of meaning is very narcissistic and crude, but I think it can be useful, when going through that kind of experience.

KEITH GESSEN: And then, I think you once told me, you would later become annoyed when you encountered undergraduates for whom it was just a given that Ishmael and Queequeg were having sex.

CALEB CRAIN: I wasn't annoyed by that, but I was sort of amazed. Only twenty years ago that was something you suspected, and that you thought of as a secret treasure that you had borne away from the novel thanks to your powers of interpretation. And now it's standard operating procedure for 18-year-olds. But that's what progress is like.

MARCO ROTH: Everybody knows already what it took us years to figure it.

KEITH GESSEN: I want to tell another story. I didn't learn about the band Pavement—again it seems to be a rock band—I didn't learn about the band Pavement until I read an obituary for them in *Feed* magazine in the year 2000. And Pavement would have made college . . . It would have made college more tolerable, but the point of the story is . . . I wish I'd known about them when they were still, you know, a band. So my question is: Who are the important writers that one ought to know about now who are still alive?

CALEB CRAIN: Well I think Alice Munro would be one for me. Alan Hollinghurst.

MARCO ROTH: Well, V. S. Naipaul is still alive. Philip Roth is still alive.

KEITH GESSEN: Which book in particular?

MARCO ROTH: *The Enigma of Arrival*. *A House for Mr. Biswas*. Don DeLillo, and, for kids going off to college, why not Edward St. Aubyn, who almost won the Booker Prize, and thoroughly should have, for *Mother's Milk*.

MEGHAN FALVEY: There's lots of heroin.

MARCO ROTH: Sorry?

MEGHAN FALVEY: There's lots of heroin in St. Aubyn. That sort of binge that Patrick Melrose goes on when he's in New York collecting his father's ashes. Well, you're not reading it for the plot anyway.

KEITH GESSEN: Living sociologists?

MEGHAN FALVEY: Oh, living sociology? Huh-ho! There are a lot of living sociologists who should be read. It's hard to narrow it down. Just off the top of my head, if you're in college and you want to find out how people get jobs later on, Mark Granovetter's *Getting a Job* will disabuse you of any notion that you can rely on your merits alone. And I know he's in my department, but Richard Sennett's books might be a good place to start because they're well written and there's no off-putting jargon.

MARCO ROTH: David Bromwich's *Politics by Other Means*, which may be the best book about the culture wars of the 1980s and early '90s. And there's a lot of college that still takes place in the aftermath of the culture wars.

CHAD HARBACH: The Norwegian philosopher Arne Naess, who's a young, sexy 95 or so, still publishing, and who might be the most important philosopher of the second half of the century. He's the founder of ecosophy, and of the deep ecology platform. Essentially, he tries to formulate an ethical philosophy that takes into account the fundamental facts of our physical life. The result is both familiar—he thinks we should live more modestly than we do—and unsettling, because if you try to think deeply about problems like overpopulation and resource apportionment, you wind up caught in some serious paradoxes. Easier to ignore this stuff, which is what we mostly do.

CALEB CRAIN: I mean I think . . . Can we put somebody like James Wood down? Or do they need to be novelists, artists?

KEITH GESSEN: You really think it's important for 18-year-olds to read James Wood.

CALEB CRAIN: Well, yes.

KEITH GESSEN: The world will do that work.

CHAD HARBACH: They're already doing it.

MARCO ROTH: Mark Greif! I think everyone should read Mark Greif—the world would be better. I think people should read Mark Greif.

KEITH GESSEN: Is there a book you should not have read?

MEGHAN FALVEY: I think I should not have read *Portrait of the Artist as a Young Man* when I did, because it was deceptively, you know, easy to read.

MARCO ROTH: When did you read it?

MEGHAN FALVEY: Well, it was a book that my parents had, my dad had, so I read it . . . I think before I was even in high school. And then I re-read it in high school. I think there are certain kinds of, like, self-righteousness and piety that, um, I have yet to root out of myself.

KEITH GESSEN: I remember my parents kept *Catcher in the Rye* from me until I turned 13.

CALEB CRAIN: Really?

KEITH GESSEN: They're like [whispering], "He can't read it until he's 13." And then I read it, and I was like, "What's the big deal?" And there's a, you know, there's a prostitute in it, in her slip.

CHAD HARBACH: The pictures of naked women in the *Sports Illustrated* Swimsuit Issue!

MEGHAN FALVEY: Isn't that issue all pictures of naked women?

CHAD HARBACH: But it didn't use to be.

MARCO ROTH: Really?

CHAD HARBACH: It's important for the young people to know that in, say, the late '80s—

CALEB CRAIN: There was a part of the *Sports Illustrated* Swimsuit Issue that was not swimsuits?

CHAD HARBACH: Right.

KEITH GESSEN: Wait, now it's all swimsuits?

CHAD HARBACH: It has been for years. But in the mid to late '80s, it was just a twenty-page section in the middle, and then there'd be an article about baseball. And my parents didn't want to deny me the articles. But this caused chaos in my soul, because I was like, "What is being withheld? What are these unbent staples?" And it turned out my whole sexual life was contained within that unbent staple.

MARCO ROTH: I think everyone who goes to college now should read the Marquis de Sade, because they're living in this age of, we're living in the age of—

CALEB CRAIN: They don't need to *read* the Marquis de Sade.

MARCO ROTH: I know, but they should, because they should learn to be disgusted by what's going on around them.

CHAD HARBACH: They *are* disgusted.

KEITH GESSEN: You talked about Henry Adams. Are there other books like that, which you'd have liked if you'd stuck with them?

CALEB CRAIN: I did that with *What Maisie Knew*, too. I totally didn't understand *What Maisie Knew* when I was 22, but it made a lot of sense when I was 35.

MARCO ROTH: Yeah, Henry James—I also had that experience. In college, the short stories were comprehensible—"In the Cage," "The Beast in the Jungle," and "The Figure in the Carpet." But then the novels took me several attempts.

CALEB CRAIN: But it has to be said, if someone had told me that that would happen when I was 18, I would not have believed them. When I was young, when I heard people saying that you have to wait until you have some experience, or until you're more mature, in order to be able to read certain things or write certain things, I was like, "That's just bullshit." It's what the economists call "rent." The people who paid their rent by surviving for a decade without doing anything important don't want anybody younger than them to skip over that period, so they're trying to keep us out, you know? Although maybe I think differently now just because I've paid my rent.

MARCO ROTH: *The Ambassadors* I tried many times to read, before really succeeding at 25.

KEITH GESSEN: Mmhmm. Would that have changed your life if you had read it earlier?

MARCO ROTH: I don't think I would have been receptive to that kind of selflessness then. Nor optimism. I'd read two essays of Emerson's in high school without making any effort to comprehend them. And then, much later, I started to re-read "Self-Reliance" and "Circles." And I thought, "Why did I read Nietzsche when I could have been reading Emerson?"

CALEB CRAIN: Oh, so the opposite.

KEITH GESSEN: Yeah, for Caleb—Emerson *was* his Nietzsche.

CALEB CRAIN: Right. Emerson was my Nietzsche.

MARCO ROTH: Would you rather have read Nietzsche than—

CALEB CRAIN: I think I read Nietzsche when I was in high school? And then I read Emerson when I was in graduate school.

KEITH GESSEN: So you lied.

CALEB CRAIN: Well, I mean, the Nietzsche didn't make anywhere near as big an impression on me as it did on you. It was the Emerson that I memorized and went around reciting to people. But, you know, I was embarrassingly old when I did that. I wasn't actually a teenager. I didn't have the social identity appropriate for doing that, but I was doing it anyway.

CHAD HARBACH: And yet our society should be constructed such that that's OK.

MARCO ROTH: Here's another regret. There are certain optimist philosophers, like Emerson, that in my case I encountered after the pessimist versions of them. And therefore hope is still an intellectual concept to me, but it's not a real thing, at all. And that may be just for other reasons that I don't yet understand, but I wonder if at 18 I'd read Emerson, you know, and really got it, then I would have . . . If I spent more time there, then I might, you know . . .

[Pause.]

CALEB CRAIN: I wish I had read Winnicott earlier. I didn't read him until halfway through grad school. It's easy to read—it's not like Melanie Klein, which is hard. Klein would also have been useful to read earlier, but I probably was only going to read her when I did. But Winnicott—it's so deceptively easy to read, but the concepts were very helpful to me.

KEITH GESSEN: So, Meghan, as a young woman, you were filled with this belief that you were forging the conscience of your race, that is to say in the smithy of your soul, which maybe you were too young to have that idea—

CALEB CRAIN: It makes sense that you would feel like you had read James Joyce too young, and then you had this identification with Edna O'Brien because—

MEGHAN FALVEY: Oh, right, yeah—

CALEB CRAIN: Because she has this whole writerly identification with James Joyce.

MARCO ROTH: Maybe that novel is really about James Joyce, like Joyce and Nora.

MEGHAN FALVEY: Huh. I don't know about that.

MARCO ROTH: Just a suggestion. I wish I hadn't learned to talk about books I haven't read!

CHAD HARBACH: I also regret that Marco did that!

KEITH GESSEN [to Meghan]: Is there a book that liberated you from that, or in general?

MEGHAN FALVEY: Oh, from—?

KEITH GESSEN: From anything, from anything.

MEGHAN FALVEY: I don't know if there was really an antidote to Joyce.

KEITH GESSEN: Well, you have a very strong political bent in your writing, so I'm interested if you could name some of the books that took you there.

MEGHAN FALVEY: Something like Richard Sennett's *The Hidden Injuries of Class* or *The Corrosion of Character*, anyone of the regulation school . . . I want to say, read about the social organization of the economy because it's going to determine a lot of the rest of your life and it should be demystified. And debunked—even if you are content with the ways things are, or your own portion of the spoils. Read Harvey, read Alain Lipietz and Michel Aglietta, except they're so dense I still feel like I'm knocking my head against a wall when I read them now.

KEITH GESSEN: Is there a David Harvey book that you would recommend?

MEGHAN FALVEY: *The Limits to Capital.* But Jamie Peck's *Workfare States* or Piven and Cloward's *Regulating the Poor* might be easier to start with. Or even, start with a novel like J. G. Farrell's *Troubles*, in which the characters don't have as much money or status or power as they want or as they used to have, as a class. And people with some kind of power often think of how they have less of it than another group, they see themselves as subject to things they can't control. Nobody wants to think of themselves as an oppressor or as a person with privilege. You know, "I'm white but I'm a good person!" And in the US these days, you're going to live on one side of the very wide gap between rich and poor, and if you are on the lucky side you should admit it. And find out why that gap exists and maybe how to distribute some pretty modest, basic goods more evenly.

CHAD HARBACH: There's a book called *The Idea of Wilderness*, by Max Oelschlaeger, which I recommend. It's a good introduction to the history of ecological thought.

KEITH GESSEN: Other left-wing books? Caleb books?

CALEB CRAIN: I don't know. What are you looking for?

KEITH GESSEN: The kind of books you think everybody should read if they want to talk to you.

CALEB CRAIN: People can talk to me. They don't have to have read a particular book.

When I was young, the authors that you had to read were the minimalists, like Raymond Carver. I'm sure there's a trend like that today that I don't even see because it's right before my eyes.

KEITH GESSEN: I think baroque, late postmodernism is what we've got now . . . and, boy, I miss Raymond Carver!

MARCO ROTH: You think kids in college are reading Jonathan Safran Foer?

KEITH GESSEN: Yeah. I think that's the equivalent.

MARCO ROTH: And Dave Eggers?

KEITH GESSEN: Dave Eggers is their Carver, and JSF is their Bobbie Ann Mason.

MFA; FINAL ADVICE

CHAD HARBACH: I feel like until the past three years or so I was always sort of reacting. I wanted to write, and this felt very important to me, and so I wrote, even though I wasn't sure exactly why. I'd just sit there with a pen in my hand, or in front of my computer, and I constructed my entire life so I could sit there. And this went on for seven years. During that time I probably earned, you know, $100,000—

KEITH GESSEN: A year?

CHAD HARBACH: In total! I can produce the Social Security forms to demonstrate this. And it's like, "Why do this?" And one can still ask this. I could have had a career! But eventually I began to feel different about it, in the sense that I felt that I was no longer reacting. I would no longer read something just because it appeared before me, but because it was what I needed to read at that time. And writing, too, became more purposeful. And so the whole project of sitting in a room—whether or not it's all that useful to the world—at least became more shaped by who I am and what I care and worry about, so that now it feels like work that needs doing.

KEITH GESSEN: All right, final question. Are there things that you have done with your life that, if you had known something at the age of 18, you would not have done?

CALEB CRAIN: I talked earlier about regretting my undergraduate career so I went to graduate school. Then after that I regretted graduate school, so I went to work at *Lingua Franca*.

KEITH GESSEN: What's *Lingua Franca*?

CALEB CRAIN: *Lingua Franca* was a magazine that covered the academic life from a journalistic angle. A certain number of young writers and editors got their start there who now . . . control the world! No, not really, but many of them are now employed at the *New York Times Book Review*, the *New York Times Magazine*, and the *New Yorker*. And a few of them never got jobs, like me.

When I left college, maybe I could have short-circuited all that ambiguity, that long road, by going to get an MFA. When I graduated, I knew I wanted to work for a year, save money, and go abroad, and I did that. But then I was like, "Should I get an MFA, or should I get a Ph.D.?"

And, to an extent, I regret getting the Ph.D. but still think it was the right thing for me to have done. Because no, I didn't become a professor. I knew I wasn't going to become a professor when I started—although I went through lots of psychic agony wondering about it along the way.

Anyway, so I wondered: What I wanted to do was write novels, so why did I go get a Ph.D., and then become a journalist and a critic, and *then* write novels? Why did I do it that way, instead of going to get an MFA, in which case I could have written the novels right away? And that's a genuine question mark, because I don't know what it would have been like for me to get an MFA. I mean, I did write novels anyway all throughout graduate school, and they were terrible. So it's possible that if novel-writing had been my major focus in my twenties and thirties, I would have nothing at all to show for those decades. Whereas now I have a Ph.D. that I don't use.

KEITH GESSEN: Chad? MFA or Ph.D.?

CHAD HARBACH: Well, I'll state for the record that I have an MFA. I just talked about my seven years of sitting in front of a piece of paper, and my MFA took up the last three of those years. You know, an MFA is a much-maligned thing in our culture. There's a lot of distrust and anxiety about MFA programs—people write trend articles about how the work that comes out of them is automatically bad. I disagree. But one should never pay for an MFA.

CALEB CRAIN: That's what decided me. I wasn't going to have to pay for the Ph.D., but I thought I was going to have to pay for the MFA.

CHAD HARBACH: In certain ways, that's what it comes down to. If you get paid to do an MFA, then this is a rare instance of state subsidy for artistic endeavor in the United States. And I think that's a good thing. But, well, it's complicated. People go to MFA programs, and they're surrounded by bad writers, and they're also thrust into this situation where, whatever they were pretending to do before, they're no longer able to pretend to be doing it. So you get to an MFA program and the people around you will be snorting a lot of coke, and having all these crises, because they've been put in this place where they finally have to produce. They've always gone around introducing themselves as writers, and now they're in this place where they have to write things.

And in a way, you get a little bit of satisfaction from showing up at an MFA program, right? You have no career, no visible means of supporting yourself, and you've been doing nothing for several years since you got out of college—this is a very deeply anxiety-inducing situation. And you have this pride that prevents you from calling yourself a writer, and so you call yourself . . . well, you might call yourself a journalist, if you're an excellent journalist, or, in my case, you could just try to avoid all human contact.

MARCO ROTH: That sounds a lot like graduate school. I mean, you're not describing a dissimilar experience.

CALEB CRAIN: It sounds like a Knut Hamsun novel.

KEITH GESSEN: ". . . and then Chad ate his own arm!"

CHAD HARBACH: So there's this brief period of happiness when you get to the MFA program, because people say, "What do you do?" And you can say, "They pay me 900 dollars a month to be here." And this is satisfying. But then that dissipates and everyone goes crazy. You get to see a lot of people go crazy in an MFA program—it's very educational. And then at the end of it, one person you know has written a successful chick-lit novel that was sold to a movie company for a million dollars, and everyone else has gone off to get a Ph.D., or has just sort of gotten married.

KEITH GESSEN: It's the *Buddenbrooks* of MFA answers! The consequences of an MFA through the generations.

CHAD HARBACH: My point is that if you get paid to get an MFA, it's a perfectly good idea, and if you get paid to get a Ph.D., that's also a perfectly good idea.

KEITH GESSEN: Well, not to be Mr. Regret over here, but I did do journalism for many years, and then I did get an MFA, and I am now at a point where I have a book that's going to come out finally. And yet, if I had not done any of that, I might have gotten to my book a lot faster, and been able to enjoy it, in a way that I'm now—

CALEB CRAIN: But what would your book have been about?

KEITH GESSEN: Something. The same thing.

CHAD HARBACH: Would that have been better? You're a man who's 32? If you had published your book four years ago?

KEITH GESSEN: I would have preferred that. It would have felt better, a youthful feeling, it would have been a part of my youth, and it would have been tied into the euphoria of youth. And now it is tied to the anxieties of middle age, of work, and of one's good name.

CALEB CRAIN: But don't you think some of those anxieties would have come to you even at age 28 upon publishing a book?

KEITH GESSEN: I have more to lose now.

MARCO ROTH: I don't know, I mean, we live in a culture now—a publishing culture, especially—where everybody gets more than one chance.

CALEB CRAIN: Where everybody gets more than one chance?

MARCO ROTH: Yeah. I mean, if you publish a first novel at 28, and then you go into hiding for seven years and come back at 35, they love that.

CALEB CRAIN: "You thought he'd fallen off the earth, and he's written a second novel!"

KEITH GESSEN: I was thinking more of losing my good name, as a respectable citizen, rather than my publishing career.

Meghan, do you have an answer?

MEGHAN FALVEY: To which question?

KEITH GESSEN: To "Ph.D., or not?"

MEGHAN FALVEY: Just hearing you speak just now, I was thinking, "Hold fast against the cult of precocity." It's all just callowness, right? When I was 27, I was like, "What have I done? Nothing." But for some reason, that anxiety ceased to have its ability to keep me up at night. I actually feel uncharacteristically, not optimistic, but rather just kind of free of the strains of one particular sort of culturally imposed period of one's life, without having done anything recognizable as entering the next one.

CALEB CRAIN: I would second that. If I were speaking to an 18-year-old, I'd say, "Don't worry. Don't be precocious." But the flip side of that is, this is the only life you'll get, and it won't come again. So, I don't think you should be precocious, and I don't think you should beat yourself up for not having published a book at the age of 28, but I think that a young person should keep a journal, and read seriously, and, you know, think about everything that happens.

—July 24, 2007

BOOKS THAT CHANGED MY LIFE

CALEB CRAIN

1. Charles Dickens, *David Copperfield* (1850)
2. Herman Melville, *Moby-Dick* (1851)
3. Václav Havel, *Disturbing the Peace* (1991)
4. Ralph Waldo Emerson, *Essays and Lectures* (1983)
5. Frank O'Hara, *Selected Poems* (1951–74)
6. James Schuyler, *Alfred and Guinevere* (1958)
7. Henry Green, *Loving* (1945)
8. Edith Wharton, *The House of Mirth* (1905)

MEGHAN FALVEY

1. Nancy Chodorow, *Feminism and Psychoanalytic Theory* (1989)
2. Nancy Folbre, *The Invisible Heart: Economics and Family Values* (2001)
3. Karl Polanyi, *The Great Transformation* (1944)
4. Jean Starobinski, *Largesse* (1994)
5. Georg Simmel, *The Philosophy of Money* (1900)
6. Jamie Peck, *Workfare States* (2001)
7. Marcel Mauss, *The Gift: Forms and Function of Exchange in Archaic Societies* (1923–24)
8. Nancy Fraser, *Justice Interrupus* (1997)

CHAD HARBACH

1. Arne Naess, *Ecology, Community and Lifestyle* (1989)
2. Bill McKibben, *The End of Nature* (1989)
3. Elizabeth Kolbert, *Field Notes from a Catastrophe* (2006)
4. Homer, *The Iliad*; *The Odyssey* (ca. 8th century BCE).
5. William Shakespeare, Plays; Sonnets (1590–1613).
6. Herman Melville, *Moby-Dick* (1851)

7. Henry David Thoreau, *Walden* (1854)
8. Anton Chekhov, *Stories*, Pevear & Volokhonsky trans. (2000); *Complete Short Novels*, Pevear & Volokhonsky trans. (2005); *Plays*, Paul Schmidt trans. (1998)
9. William Faulkner, *The Sound and the Fury* (1929); *As I Lay Dying* (1930); *Absalom, Absalom!* (1936)
10. David Foster Wallace, *Infinite Jest* (1996)

MARCO ROTH

1. Thomas Mann, *Tonio Kroger* (1903)
2. Soren Kierkegaard, *Either/Or*, vol I (1843)
3. W. B. Yeats, *Collected Poems* (1889–1939)
4. Fyodor Dostoevsky, *Crime and Punishment* (1866)
5. Henry James, *The Ambassadors* (1903)
6. Harold Bloom, *The Anxiety of Influence* (1973)
7. V. S. Naipaul, *The Enigma of Arrival* (1987)
8. Max Horkheimer & Theodor W. Adorno, *The Dialectic of Enlightenment* (1944)

KEITH GESSEN

1. Honoré de Balzac, *Lost Illusions* (1837–39)
2. Leo Tolstoy, *War and Peace* (1865–69)
3. Don DeLillo, *White Noise* (1985)
4. Joseph Brodsky, *Less Than One: Selected Essays* (1986)
5. Michel Houellebecq, *Elementary Particles* (1998)
6. Thomas Frank and Matt Weiland, eds. *Commodify Your Dissent* (1997)
7. Irving Howe, *A Margin of Hope* (1982)
8. Philip Roth, *Zuckerman Bound* (1979–85); *Sabbath's Theater* (1995)
9. Adam Ulam, *The Bolsheviks* (1965)
10. Saul Bellow, *Herzog* (1965); *Humboldt's Gift* (1975)

N EARLY ALL THE PARTICIPANTS, when shown the transcripts of the panels, expressed embarrassment and chagrin. "I have pleasant memories of our discussion," wrote Ilya Bernstein, "but when I read over what I said just now, it sounded like gibberish and platitudes. I probably rely on body language more than I knew." Chad Harbach and Benjamin Kunkel registered dismay at what seemed to them their inarticulateness. Kate Bolick and Marco Roth suggested that their contributions could be cut entirely. "I took out most of the 'likes' and 'you knows' your very hard-working intern [Andrew Jacobs] attributed to me," wrote Siddhartha Deb, from India, "because I believe I do not use them, like, at all."

As moderator, I strongly disagree. I do think it's an open question just how central the central debates of our own college years still are—the canon versus multiculturalism; Theory versus empiricism; the Frankfurt School versus poststructuralism, and both of them versus Anglo-American philosophy—though

I suspect they haven't gone away. But I am certain that the most valuable parts of these talks lie beyond those debates. They are the moments when the panelists reveal their deep uncertainty—Meghan Falvey walking in a mist of abstraction on the way to her dorm from Phenomenology, Existentialism, and something else with a P—and how each of them has struggled to read and think their way out of that uncertainty. It turns out that in order to become an intellectual, you must first become a pseudo-intellecutal. But to have the courage, in the meantime, of your uncertainty—to remain open to things, and serious about them—would be a pretty good way to go through college, and not just college.

Good luck.

—Keith Gessen

Ackerley, J. R. *My Father and Myself* (1968).

Adams, Henry. *The Education of Henry Adams* (1907).

Althusser, Louis. *For Marx* (1965); "Ideology and Ideological State Apparatuses," in *Lenin and Philosophy and Other Essays* (1971).

Amin, Ash. *Post-Fordism: a Reader* (1994).

Anderson, Perry. *Considerations on Western Marxism* (1976); *Zone of Engagement* (1992); *Spectrum* (2006).

Aron, Raymond. *Main Currents in Sociological Thought*, 2 vol., (1965).

Balzac. *Lost Illusions* (1837–39).

Barthelme, Donald. *40 Stories* (1987).

Baudelaire, Charles. *Flowers of Evil* (1857).

Bayly, Christopher Alan. *The Birth of the Modern World: Global Connections and Comparisons*, 1780–1914 (2004).

Bedford, Sybille. *A Legacy* (1956).

Bhimsain. *Gharonda* (1977).

Bishop, Elizabeth. *Complete Poems* (1969).

Blake, William. *Poems and Prophecies* (1783–1820).

Bolaño, Roberto. *Distant Star* (1996); *The Savage Detectives* (1998); *By Night in Chile* (2000).

Bromwich, David. *Politics by Other Means: Higher Education and Group Thinking* (1992).

Burgess, Anthony. *99 Novels: The Best in English Since 1939—A Personal Choice* (1984).

Burroughs, William S. *Naked Lunch* (1959).

Carver, Raymond. *Will You Please Be Quiet, Please?* (1976); *What We Talk About When We Talk About Love* (1981).

Cavell, Stanley. *Must We Mean What We Say?* (1969); *The World Viewed* (1971); *The Senses of Walden* (1972); *Pursuits of Happiness* (1981); *Conditions Handsome and Unhandsome* (1990); *Contesting Tears* (1996).

Chaucer, Geoffrey. *Canterbury Tales* (1387–1400).

Chuang Tzu. *Zhuangzi* (ca. 4th century BCE).

Confucius. *Analects* (ca. 3-6th centuries BCE).

Dartmouth Review. Combative right-wing student publication (1980–present).

Das, Jibanananda. *Collected Poems* (1985–96).

Deleuze, Gilles. *Proust and Signs* (1964).

DeLillo, Don. *End Zone* (1972); *Great Jones Street* (1973); *Players* (1977); *White Noise* (1985); *Mao II* (1991).

Dickens, Charles. *David Copperfield* (1850).

Duras, Marguerite. *The Lover* (1984).

Eagleton, Terry. *The Gatekeeper: A Memoir* (2001).

Eco, Umberto. *The Name of the Rose* (1980).

Eggers, Dave. *A Heartbreaking Work of Staggering Genius* (2000); *What Is the What: The Autobiography of Valentino Achak Deng* (2006)

Ellison, Ralph. *Invisible Man* (1952).

Emerson, Ralph Waldo. *Essays: First Series* (1841).

Farrell, J. G. *Troubles* (1970); *The Siege of Krishnapur* (1973); *The Singapore Grip* (1978).

Feed. Early online magazine of culture and technology (1995–2000).

Flaubert, Gustave. *Madame Bovary* (1857); *Sentimental Education* (1869).

Foer, Jonathan Safran (also, "JSF"). *Everything Is Illuminated* (2002).

Foucault, Michel. *The Order of Things: An Archaeology of Human Sciences* (1966); "What is an Author" (1971; collected in *The Foucault Reader*, 1984); *Discipline and Punish* (1975); *The History of Sexuality Vol. 1: An Introduction* (1976); *The History of Sexuality Vol. 2: The Uses of Pleasure* (1984); *Foucault Live: Interviews, 1961–84* (1996).

Fox, Paula. *Desperate Characters* (1970).

Frye, Northrop. *Fearful Symmetry: A Study of William Blake* (1947); *Anatomy of Criticism* (1957).

Fukuyama, Francis. *The End of History and the Last Man* (1992).

Gallant, Mavis. *The Collected Stories of Mavis Gallant* (1996).

Ginsberg, Allen. *Howl and Other Poems* (1956).

Goethe, Johann Wolfgang von. *The Sorrows of Young Werther* (1774)

Gorz, Andre. *Farewell to the Working Class: An Essay on Post-Industrial Socialism* (1980).

Granovetter, Mark. *Getting a Job: A Study of Contacts and Careers* (1995).

Green, Henry. *Loving* (1945).

Hamsun, Kurt. *Hunger* (1890).

Hardy, Thomas. *Jude the Obscure* (1895).

Hartley, L. P. *The Go-Between* (1953).

Harvey, David. *The Limits to Capital* (1999).

Hayek, F. A. *The Road to Serfdom* (1944).

Hegel, Georg Wilhelm Friedrich. *Phenomenology of Spirit* (1807).

Hobbes, Thomas. *Leviathan* (1660).

Hobsbawm, Eric. *The Age of Revolution* (1962); *The Age of Capital* (1975); *The Age of Empire* (1987).

Hollinghurst, Alan. *The Line of Beauty* (2004).

Homer. *Iliad*; *Odyssey* (ca. 8th century BCE).

Horkheimer, Max and Theodor W. Adorno. *Dialectic of Enlightenment* (1944).

Houellebecq, Michel. *Whatever* (1994); *The Elementary Particles* (1998).

James, Henry. *The Portrait of a Lady* (1881); "The Figure in the Carpet" (1896); "What Maisie Knew" (1897); "In the Cage" (1898); "The Beast in the Jungle" (1903); *The Ambassadors* (1903).

Jameson, Frederic. *The Prison-House of Language: A Critical Account of Structuralism and Russian Formalism* (1972); *Fables of Aggression: Wyndham Lewis, the Modernist as Fascist* (1979); *Postmodernism, or, The Cultural Logic of Late Capitalism* (1991).

Joyce, James. *Portrait of the Artist as a Young Man* (1916).

Kant, Immanuel. *Critique of Judgment* (1790).

Kapoor, Raj. *Mera Naam Joker* (1970).

Keats, John. "Ode on Melancholy," "Ode on a Grecian Urn," "Ode to a Nightingale," "To Autumn," "On seeing the Elgin Marbles," "Lamia," *Letters* (1814–19).

Kerouac, Jack. *On the Road* (1957).

Kierkegaard, Soren. *Either/Or* (1843).; *Fear and Trembling* (1843).

Klein, Melanie. "A Contribution to the Psychogenesis of Manic-Depressive States" in *The Selected Melanie Klein* (1987).

Kripke, Saul. *Naming and Necessity* (1972).

Kundera, Milan. *The Book of Laughter and Forgetting* (1979); *The Unbearable Lightness of Being* (1984). But see also: *The Joke* (1967).

Lao Tzu. *Laozi* (ca. 4–6th centuries BCE).

Lawrence, D. H. *Sons and Lovers* (1913); *The Rainbow* (1915).

Lingua Franca. Magazine that reported on trends and personalities in academic life (1990-2001).

Lenin, Vladimir Ilyich. *What is to Be Done?* (1902); *The State and Revolution* (1917).

Locke, John. *Two Treatises of Government* (1690).

Lovelock, James. *Gaia* (1979); *The Revenge of Gaia* (2006).

de Man, Paul. *Blindness and Insight: Essays in the Rhetoric of Contemporary Criticism* (1983).

Mann, Thomas. *Buddenbrooks* (1901).

Marx, Karl. *The Communist Manifesto* (1848); *The Eighteenth Brumaire of Louis Bonaparte* (1852); *A Contribution to the Critique of Political Economy* (1859).

Mason, Bobbie Ann. *Shiloh and Other Stories* (1982).

McCarthy, Mary. *The Company She Keeps* (1942); *Memories of a Catholic Girlhood* (1957); *The Group* (1962); *Intellectual Memoirs* (1992); *A Bolt from the Blue and Other Essays* (2002).

Mehra, Prakesh. *Muqaddar ka Sikandar* (1978).

Melville, Herman. *Moby-Dick* (1851); *The Piazza Tales* (1856); *Billy Budd* (1886–91).

Mencius. *Mencius* (ca. 4th century BCE).

Michaels, Leonard. *I Would Have Saved Them If I Could* (1975).

Miller, Henry. *Tropic of Cancer* (1934); *Tropic of Capricorn* (1938)

Milton, John. *Paradise Lost* (1667).

Munro, Alice. *Carried Away: Selected Stories* (2006).

Musil, Robert. *A Man Without Qualities* (1930–33).

Naess, Arne. *Ecology, Community and Lifestyle* (1989); *Deep Ecology for the 21st Century*, ed. George Sessions (1995).

Naipaul, V. S. *A House for Mr. Biswas* (1961); *The Enigma of Arrival* (1987). See also: *Bend in the River* (1979).

Nandy, Ashish. *The Savage Freud and Other Essays on Possible and Retrievable Selves* (1995).

New Left Review. Mighty magazine of Marxist critical theory, aesthetics, history, economics, (1960–present).

Nicholson, Linda. *The Play of Reason: From the Modern to the Postmodern* (1999).

Nietzsche, Friedrich. *The Birth of Tragedy* (1872). *The Gay Science* (1882); *Beyond Good and Evil* (1886); *Human, All-Too-Human* (1886); *On the Genealogy of Morals* (1887).

O'Brien, Edna. *The Country Girls* (1960); *Girls in Their Married Bliss* (1964).

Oelschlaeger, Max. *The Idea of Wilderness* (1991).

Offe, Claus and John Keane. *Contradictions of the Welfare State* (1984)

Ondaatje, Michael. *The English Patient* (1992).

Pavement. *Crooked Rain, Crooked Rain* (1994); *Slanted and Enchanted* (1992); *Wowee Zowee* (1995); *Brighten the Corners* (1997). See also: The Silver Jews, *American Water* (1998).

Peck, James. *Workfare States* (2001).

Pinker, Robert. *The Idea of Welfare* (1979).

Piven, Francis Fox and Richard Cloward. *Regulating the Poor* (1971).

Plato. *The Republic* (360 BCE).

Poirier, Richard. "Venerable Complications: Literature, Technology, and People" in *The Renewal of Literature* (1987).

Pontecorvo, Gillo. *Burn!* (1969). See also: *Battle of Algiers* (1965).

Pynchon, Thomas. *Gravity's Rainbow* (1973).

Quine, W. V. O. *From a Logical Point of View* (1953).

Rand, Ayn. *The Fountainhead* (1943); *Atlas Shrugged* (1957).

Rawls, John. *Theory of Justice* (1971).

Roth, Philip. *Portnoy's Complaint* (1969); *The Ghost Writer* (1979); *Zuckerman Unbound* (1981); *The Anatomy Lesson* (1983); *The Prague Orgy* (1985); *The Counterlife* (1986); *The Facts: A Novelist's Autobiography* (1988); *Operation Shylock: A Confession* (1993); *Sabbath's Theater* (1995).

de Sade, Marquis. *120 Days of Sodom* (1780s); *Philosophy in the Bedroom* (1795). Marco Roth: "This entry should read: As much as they can stand or until they get bored."

Saint-Exupery, Antoine de. *The Little Prince* (1943).

Salinger, J. D. *The Catcher in the Rye* (1951).

Samanta, Shakti. *Amanush* (1975).

Saramago, José. *Blindness* (1995). See also: *The Year of the Death of Ricardo Reis* (1986).

Saunders, George. *CivilWarLand in Bad Decline* (1996); *Pastoralia* (2000).

Schopenhauer, Arthur. *The World as Will and Representation* (1818).

Schumpeter, Joseph. *Capitalism, Socialism, and Democracy* (1942).

Sebald, W. G. *Vertigo* (1990); *The Emigrants* (1993); *Rings of Saturn* (1995); *Austerlitz* (2001).

Sennett, Richard. *The Hidden Injuries of Class* (1993); *The Corrosion of Character* (1998).

Shakespeare, William. *Coriolanus* (1608).

Shelley, Percy Bysshe. "On Life"; "Hymn to Intellectual Beauty"; "Julian and Maddalo"; "Ode to the West Wind"; "Prometheus Unbound"; "Triumph of Life"; "A Defense of Poetry" (1815–1840).

Singer, Isaac Bashevis. *Enemies: A Love Story* (1972); *The Collected Stories of Isaac Bashevis Singer* (1982).

Spark, Muriel. *The Girls of Slender Means* (1963).

St. Aubyn, Edward. *Mother's Milk* (2006).

Stendhal. *The Red and The Black* (1830).

Straus, Leo. *Persecution and the Art of Writing* (1952).

Tacitus. *Annals of Imperial Rome* (ca. 100).

Thoreau, Henry David. "Civil Disobedience" (1849); *Walden* (1854); "A Plea for Captain John Brown" (1859); "Walking" (1861); "Life without Principle" (1863).

Tse-tung, Mao. *Quotations from Chairman Mao Tse-tung* (1964).

Uris, Leon. *Exodus* (1958).

Velvet Underground, The. *The Velvet Underground and Nico* (1967); *White Light/White Heat* (1968); *The Velvet Underground* (1969); *VU* (1985).

Welch, Denton. *Maiden Voyage* (1973).

Wharton, Edith. *The House of Mirth* (1905).

Wilson, Edmund. *The Triple Thinkers* (1938).

Winnicott, D. W. "Ego Distortion in Terms of True and False Self" in *Maturational Processes and the Facilitating Environment* (1965).

Wittgenstein, Ludwig. *Tractatus Logico-Philosophicus* (1921); *Philosophical Investigations* (1953).

Wood, James. *The Broken Estate: Essays on Literature and Belief* (1999); *The Irresponsible Self: On Laughter and the Novel* (2004).

Woolf, Virginia. *Mrs. Dalloway* (1925); *To the Lighthouse* (1927); *The Diary of Virginia Woolf*, 5 volumes (1984).

Wordsworth, William. *Lyrical Ballads, With a Few Other Poems* (1798).

Wouk, Herman. *The Caine Mutiny* (1951); *This is My God* (1959).